CW00857619

4) 76

THOMAS MÜNTZER

By the same author

FREIBURG AND THE BREISGAU: Town–Country Relations in
  the Age of Reformation and Peasants' War
DIE FREIBURGER ENQUETE VON 1476 (*editor*)
*POLITICS AND SOCIETY IN REFORMATION EUROPE (*editor
  with E. I. Kouri*)

**Also published by Macmillan*

Thomas Müntzer

Theology and Revolution
in the German Reformation

Tom Scott
Senior Lecturer in History
University of Liverpool

MACMILLAN

© Tom Scott 1989

All rights reserved. No reproduction, copy or transmission
of this publication may be made without written permission.

No paragraph of this publication may be reproduced, copied
or transmitted save with written permission or in accordance
with the provisions of the Copyright Act 1956 (as amended),
or under the terms of any licence permitting limited copying
issued by the Copyright Licensing Agency, 33–4 Alfred Place,
London WC1E 7DP.

Any person who does any unauthorised act in relation to
this publication may be liable to criminal prosecution and
civil claims for damages.

First published 1989

Published by
MACMILLAN PRESS LTD
Houndmills, Basingstoke, Hampshire RG21 2XS
and London
Companies and representatives
throughout the world

Printed in Hong Kong

British Library Cataloguing-in-Publication Data
Scott, Tom. 1947 –
Thomas Müntzer
1. Anabaptist churches. Müntzer, Thomas ca. 1490–1525
I. Title.
284'.3'0924
ISBN 0–333–46498–2

In memoriam
Ernesti Gordoni Rupp
mentoris
inter theologorum furorem
εἰρηνικωτάτου

Contents

List of Maps and Figures

List of Abbreviations

AGBM II   *Akten zur Geschichte des Bauernkriegs in Mittel-deutschland*, ed. Walther Peter Fuchs, vol. II (Jena, 1942; reprint Aalen, 1964)

B   Manfred Bensing, *Thomas Müntzer und der Thüringer Aufstand 1525* (Leipziger Übersetzungen und Abhandlungen zum Mittelalter, series B III) (Berlin, 1966)

CW   *The Collected Works of Thomas Müntzer*, ed. Peter Matheson (Edinburgh, 1988)

E   Walter Elliger, *Thomas Müntzer. Leben und Werk*, 2nd edn (Göttingen, 1975)

F   *Thomas Müntzer. Schriften und Briefe. Kritische Gesamtausgabe*, ed. Günther Franz (Quellen und Forschungen zur Reformationsgeschichte, XXXIII) (Gütersloh, 1968)

G I/II   *Akten und Briefe zur Kirchenpolitik Herzog Georgs von Sachsen*, 2 vols, ed. Felician Geß (Schriften der Sächsischen Kommission für Geschichte, X/XXII) (Leipzig, 1905; Leipzig/Berlin, 1917; reprint Cologne/Vienna, 1985 [= Mitteldeutsche Forschungen, Sonderreihe: Quellen und Darstellungen in Nachdrucken, VI, 1/2])

J   *Chronik der Stadt Mühlhausen in Thüringen*, ed. Reinhard Jordan, vol. I (Mühlhausen, 1900)

LW   *Luther's Works*, ed. Jaroslav Pelikan and Helmut

T. Lehmann, 55 vols (Philadelphia/St Louis, 1955ff.)

NM   Carl Eduard Förstemann (ed.), 'Zur Geschichte des Bauernkriegs im Thüringischen und Mansfeldischen', *Neue Mittheilungen aus dem Gebiet historisch-antiquarischer Forschungen*, XII (1869), 150–244

QBK   *Quellen zur Geschichte des Bauernkrieges*, ed. Günther Franz (*Ausgewählte Quellen zur Deutschen Geschichte der Neuzeit*, ed. Rudolf Buchner, vol. II) (Darmstadt, 1963)

R   Gordon Rupp, 'Thomas Müntzer. The Reformer as Rebel' in idem, *Patterns of Reformation* (London, 1969), 155–353

S I/II/III   *Urkundenbuch der Stadt Freiburg im Breisgau*, new series: *Der deutsche Bauernkrieg. Gleichzeitige Urkunden*, ed. Johann Heinrich Schreiber, 3 vols (Freiburg im Breisgau, 1863–66)

W   Eike Wolgast, *Thomas Müntzer. Ein Verstörer der Ungläubigen* (*Persönlichkeit und Geschichte*, ed. Günther Franz, vol. CXI/CXII) (Göttingen/ Zürich, 1981)

Acknowledgements

The historian who steps into the minefield of Reformation theology, especially in search of a figure as explosive as Thomas Müntzer, needs all the guidance he can get. It has been my singular fortune that scholars from many backgrounds and persuasions have been unstintingly helpful with advice and information: in the United Kingdom, Dr C. H. Clough (Liverpool), Dr H. J. Cohn (Coventry), and Dr R. W. Scribner (Cambridge); in the Republic of Ireland, Dr Michael Laffan and Dr Helga Robinson-Hammerstein (Dublin); in Canada, Prof. W. O. Packull (Waterloo, Ont.) and Prof. J. M. Stayer (Kingston, Ont.); in the United States of America, Prof. Michael Baylor (Bethlehem, Pa.) and Prof. Susan Karant-Nunn (Portland, Ore.); in the Federal Republic of Germany, Prof. Ulrich Bubenheimer (Heidelberg), Prof. Klaus Deppermann (Freiburg im Breisgau), Prof. Gottfried Seebaß and Prof. Eike Wolgast (Heidelberg); in the German Democratic Republic, Dr Siegfried Bräuer (Berlin), Dr Gerhard Günther (Mühlhausen/Thuringia), Dr Wieland Held and Prof. Siegfried Hoyer (Leipzig), Dr Manfred Kobuch (Dresden) and Prof. Günter Vogler (Berlin).

Financial assistance from the University of Liverpool and the British Council (in the form of a Cultural Exchange Fellowship to East Germany in 1986) enabled me to consult primary materials in the State Archives in Dresden and Weimar, and in the *Kreisarchiv* Mühlhausen; to the directors and staff of these institutions I am grateful for assistance and co-operation. Permission to cite extracts from the American edition of *Luther's Works* was kindly granted by Fortress Press, Philadelphia. A special acknowledgement is due to Dr Geoffrey Green, director of the publishers T. & T. Clark (Edinburgh), for his extraordinary kindness in making available the galley-proofs of Peter Matheson's English edition of Müntzer's *Collected Works*, and in allowing me to quote from it without restriction. My greatest debt, however, is owed to three colleagues and friends who read the text in its entirety and offered valuable suggestions and corrections: Prof. Hans-Jürgen Goertz (Hamburg), Rev. Prof. Peter Matheson (Dunedin), and Dr Michael Palmer (Manchester). Prof. Matheson, moreover, allowed me to consult his edition in typescript, as well as placing his expertise and wisdom at my disposal – a gesture of generosity more often sought than found in the international community of scholarship. Needless to say, they are not to blame for the errors that remain. In his struggle against the self-righteous complacency and arrogance of men of learning, exposure to error, the willingness to concede mistakes, was for Müntzer a prerequisite of the arduous journey along the stony path to truth. On the quincentenary of his birth may that lesson not go unheeded.

T. S.
Liverpool

Note on Style

Quotations from Scripture contained in the *Collected Works* retain that style; elsewhere I have used the Authorised (King James) Version. Proper names are given in German, except for sovereign princes and the German emperors. That applies even to vassals of the princes who possessed *Reichsstandschaft* (a seat in the imperial diet), for example, the counts of Mansfeld, Stolberg and Schwarzburg. Except where commonly accepted English forms exist, place names are rendered according to modern national usage, though the German forms of Czech names are given in brackets.

Note on Style

Introduction

Through the thickets of Reformation controversy Thomas Müntzer has commonly been stalked as dangerous yet exhilarating prey, arousing in the hunter dread and fascination in equal measure. No other religious revolutionary in the early years of the German Reformation struck so resonant a chord; yet none was so vilified during his lifetime or so excoriated after his death. Around his persona there swiftly arose a mighty historiographical legend, sedulously propagated by his enemies, which was designed to ridicule his visionary beliefs and to anathematise his theological doctrines. His antagonists, both Catholic and Protestant, looked upon him with a mixture of loathing and horror: he was a demon, a Beelzebub who had seduced simple men into wanton and illegitimate rebellion. Yet Müntzer's championship of the rebels of his native Saxony during the Peasants' War of 1525 makes it imperative that his thought and action should not be left to theologians and church historians alone. For in Müntzer theology and revolution, theory and practice, were uniquely and inextricably combined. To emphasise his theology at the expense of his involvement in civil rebellion is just as mistaken as to underplay his theological righteousness in favour of portraying him as the forerunner of revolutionary class consciousness.

In embracing the immanent consequences of his

theology Müntzer was, in any case, pursuing to its logical but drastic conclusion the salient conviction which distinguished all radical reformers from their more moderate counterparts: the belief that only the recreation of the early apostolic Church, guided by the Holy Spirit, could restore true faith throughout Christendom.[1] In his fundamental concern, therefore, Müntzer was neither a wilful nor an eccentric figure; on the contrary, the charges of fanaticism and incoherence so frequently levelled against him serve only to obscure the common roots he shared with other reformers. Above all, it is Müntzer's maddeningly incomplete biography which largely accounts for the difficulty in tracing those roots. Only very recently has detailed local research begun to piece together the jigsaw of his early upbringing and theological training. What stands out, as a result, is Müntzer's extraordinary synthetic power, his ability to absorb and reconcile multifarious strands of inspiration into a distinctive personal theology. He succeeded in sublating mysticism (which assumes the essential unity of man and God) and spiritualism (which affirms that the gulf between God and man can only be bridged by the Holy Spirit)[2] in a new synthesis which he embedded in an understanding of creation framed by humanist intellectual categories and a reading of history derived from biblical apocalypticism – a bewitching amalgam of bewildering variety.

The present biography, intended as an introduction to Müntzer's life and work, seeks to explain the complexity and richness of his thought in the context of his unfolding career. It explicitly assumes, therefore, that Müntzer's theology cannot be divorced from his active career – his ministry, his liturgical reforms and, ultimately, his commitment to violent rebellion. It is the work of a historian, not a theologian, writing for the former rather than the latter. Should that provoke the theologians' wrath, the author may at least take comfort in Müntzer's own remarks anent the learned biblicists.

Notes

1. Cf. Gottfried Seebaß, 'Der "linke Flügel der Reformation" ' in Kurt Löcher (ed.), *Martin Luther und die Reformation in Deutschland. Vorträge zur Ausstellung im Germanischen Nationalmuseum Nürnberg 1983* (Schriften des Vereins für Reformationsgeschichte, CXCIV) (=Wissenschaftliche Beibände zum Anzeiger des Germanischen Nationalmuseums, VIII), n.d., n.p. [Nuremberg, 1987], 123.
2. Cf. Werner O. Packull, *Mysticism and the Early South-German-Austrian Anabaptist Movement* (Studies in Anabaptist and Mennonite History, XIX) (Scottdale, Pa./Kitchener, Ont., 1977), 30.

1

Early Years

Thomas Müntzer's early years are utterly obscure. Nothing is known of him until he went to study at the university of Frankfurt an der Oder in late 1512. There he was inscribed as 'Thomas Muntczer Stolbergensis'. Upon that solitary fact hinges the reconstruction of his entire youth and early career. He was, by his own attestation, a native of the small town of Stolberg in the Harz mountains,[1] which lay in the diocese of Halberstadt on the western fringes of Saxony. Only a few miles to the east, in Eisleben, Martin Luther, subsequently his most vehement opponent, had been born in 1483. Unlike Luther's, Müntzer's birthdate is unknown. Reckoning back from his first appointment as a chantry priest in Brunswick in 1514, we can estimate that he must have been born no later than 1491, since the lowest age for ordination was customarily twenty-four. 1489 has been most frequently suggested as his year of birth, since Müntzer is supposed to have studied in Leipzig from the winter semester of 1506 onwards, and that university's statutes precluded admission to the bachelor of arts degree before the age of seventeen. On the assumption that he was christened after the nearest saint's day, Müntzer is likely to have been born around 21 December, the feast of St Thomas.

A birthdate around 1489 chimes well with our image of the fiery young reforming radical of the 1520s, but it is

1

quite possible that Müntzer was in fact much older,
having perhaps been born as early as 1467/8. Admittedly
that would have made him an unusually mature student
in his Frankfurt days; moreover, his father, who was still
alive in 1521, and his mother, who died around 1520,
would both have been in their early seventies by the time
of Müntzer's public career. A date in the 1480s, therefore,
does seem the most plausible. Unfortunately, we know
next to nothing about Müntzer's parents, not even their
first names. A family called Muntzer or Montzer (in Low
German Munter) is recorded in Stolberg throughout the
fifteenth century, and relatives can be traced to the neighbouring towns of Quedlinburg, Aschersleben and Halberstadt. The name Müntzer itself may indicate that members
of his family were engaged in minting at Stolberg, but the
Matthias Montzer who sat as a councillor there in 1491
and was master of the mint in 1497/8 cannot have been
his father, since he was dead by 1501, whereas Müntzer's
father was still alive as late as 1521. The most that can be
said, in the light of recent research on Müntzer's circle of
friends in Brunswick, is that amongst his forebears there
may well have been minters and goldsmiths.[2] If that were
the case, Müntzer's social milieu would have been situated amongst the more prosperous craftsmen and lesser
entrepreneurs in the Stolberg area whose trade may have
encouraged them to dabble in the early Saxon mining
boom. The similarities with Luther's social origins would
then be quite remarkable. Müntzer's mother, at any rate,
seems to have brought some wealth into the marriage,
judging by the rather squalid quarrel over her legacy
between father and son after her death. In the end the
inheritance did pass to Müntzer, and, whilst it is tempting
to think that it made possible his extraordinary bout of
book-buying in late 1519 and early 1520, his mother in
fact probably died later that year or even in 1521. What-

ever she may have bequeathed, by 1523 Müntzer was again on his uppers.

About Müntzer's childhood we can only speculate. He presumably attended the local school in Stolberg from the age of seven. The imagery of cataracts of water and rushing of waves which runs through his writings may echo a memory of the great deluge and destruction which is known to have befallen Stolberg in 1495. Later the family is supposed to have moved to the larger town of Quedlinburg, in whose Latin school Müntzer continued his education. The only evidence for this rests upon an entry in the Leipzig university rolls for the winter of 1506, which list eleven names from the Saxon 'nation', amongst them one 'Thomas Munczer de Quedlinburgk'. While it is perfectly possible that Müntzer was described by his domicile rather than his birthplace (as in Luther's case), he certainly regarded himself as a Stolberger. Because the Müntzer family in Stolberg is known to have had relations in Quedlinburg, however, the Leipzig matriculation may refer to a quite different Thomas Müntzer.

Doubts over the Leipzig entry in turn raise awkward questions about the course of Müntzer's academic career. At various times he acquired – or claimed to have acquired – the degrees of bachelor of arts, master of arts, and bachelor of theology. Not one of these degrees is recorded in any surviving German university graduation list. In Leipzig 'Thomas Müntzer from Quedlinburg' (whoever he may have been) must have left without taking a degree – in itself nothing unusual in those days – since his name is missing from the promotion lists. We know that Müntzer was a master of arts by the summer of 1515, since he was addressed as such in a letter from one of his Brunswick contacts.[3] That, of course, presumes an earlier bachelor's degree, but neither of these can he have acquired in Frankfurt an der Oder, because from his matriculation in late 1512 too little time had elapsed for

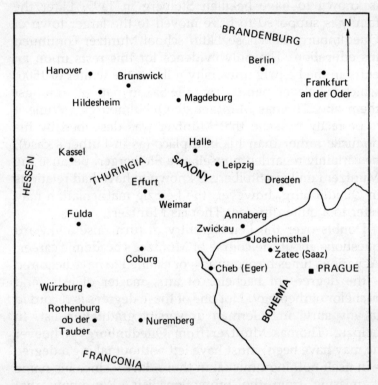

MAP 1   Central Germany in 1500

him to have completed the prescribed course of study for *both* qualifications, especially since he cannot have been in continuous residence throughout the period because of his sojourns in Aschersleben and Halle; in any case, his name again does not appear in the list of arts faculty graduates. Notwithstanding that, there seems little reason to call Müntzer's master's degree into question, since he was repeatedly so designated by his correspondents from 1515 onwards. Less certain, by contrast, is his entitlement to a bachelorship of theology. It is conceivable that he could have gained it at Frankfurt (the theology graduation lists are lost), though another five years' study was usually required after the first degree. It was once suggested that Müntzer simply assumed the title to demonstrate his theological knowledge, for it is mentioned only twice in his career, on both occasions during his stay in Zwickau. But since one instance occurs in a formal Latin greeting, probably addressed to the town council of Prague, this idea must be regarded as rather far-fetched. All these difficulties point rather to a period of study at a still unidentified third university, presumably (though not necessarily) between his Leipzig and Frankfurt semesters. Perhaps he even studied abroad.

What prompted Müntzer to choose Frankfurt as a place of study, only founded as a territorial university by the margraves of Brandenburg in 1500 and hence a mere six years senior to the electoral Saxon foundation at Wittenberg, is quite unknown. Because it lay beyond the frontiers of Saxony, some speculation has arisen, fuelled by allusions in his confession that as a youth he had taken part in conspiracies in Aschersleben and Halle, that he may have been forced to flee Saxon territory.[4] Such a conjecture goes well beyond what the sources can reasonably bear. Given our knowledge of Müntzer's theological development, there were certainly no compelling intellectual grounds for choosing Frankfurt. Just as in Leipzig, the

Frankfurt arts faculty embraced the traditional scholastic learning of the later Middle Ages founded upon Aristotle's philosophic method. By that same token, the higher faculty of divinity was committed to the realism of St Thomas Aquinas, the philosophic and theological endeavour to reconcile reason and belief. Nothing could have been further from Müntzer's subsequent understanding of a mystically experienced faith. There is, in fact, no direct evidence that Müntzer ever studied divinity at university, and in his bilious denunciations of the Wittenberg reformers as scribes and pharisees who made the dead letter of Scripture the template of religious understanding we may be hearing resonances of a sense of inferiority towards those who had enjoyed a formal theological training.

From early days, however, his intention to become a priest was manifest.[5] By his own account Müntzer had been an assistant teacher in Aschersleben and Halle in his youth, though whether he was employed in church or school (or both) is not clear. This activity probably preceded his study in Frankfurt; at all events, it cannot be dated any later than 1513, the year in which Ernest of Saxony, the archbishop of Magdeburg, against whom he confessed to having formed a 'league' in those towns, had died. The nature of this league remains entirely shadowy; it probably amounted to no more than a group of partisans whose anticlericalism challenged the spiritual and temporal authority of the archbishop. Around that time Müntzer must have been ordained, for on 6 May the following year he was presented to a chantry at the altar of the Blessed Virgin in St Michael's, Brunswick, by the Old Town city council with the duty of saying masses for the dead. The deed of appointment described him as priest in the diocese of Halberstadt. With the appointment in Brunswick we are at last on firmer ground in tracking the vagaries of Müntzer's early career.

We now know that Müntzer did indeed take up this poorly paid post in Brunswick, and for a time he shared a dwelling (and a cook) with another chantry-priest at the same altar.⁶ Although his residence was by no means continuous – at intervals he took up more attractive clerical appointments elsewhere, leaving a deputy to discharge his duties – Müntzer spent a fair stretch in Brunswick. Whilst he probably left the city for good in 1517, he did not formally resign his chantry until 1522. In Brunswick there was an active circle of pious layfolk committed to biblical humanism which took its inspiration from the *Devotio Moderna* which flourished in the late medieval Netherlands.⁷ It comprised not so much intellectuals as leading citizens engaged in trade and commerce – international merchants of the Hanseatic league (several with contacts in the Low Countries), haberdashers, drapers and brewers, some of whom sat on the council. With these men and their family networks in other cities Müntzer developed close ties which outlasted his Brunswick years. Amongst them there recur with striking frequency the names of goldsmiths, a chain of connections which can be traced to Wittenberg, Nordhausen, Allstedt, Mühlhausen and even Nuremberg. Out of the pious spiritualism of Müntzer's Brunswick friends grew dissatisfaction with the venal practices of the late medieval Catholic Church. At its core lay disillusion at the selling of indulgences.

The preaching of indulgences had been commonplace in the city during the later fifteenth century and in 1517 the St Peter's indulgence, proclaimed by pope Leo X to build the cathedral at Rome, was preached in Brunswick by, it appears, Johann Tetzel, the Dominican friar whose success in drumming-up sales of pardons inspired Luther's denunciation in the *Ninety-Five Theses*. That Müntzer took part in the indulgence controversy is evident from an undated letter he received, probably in

the summer of 1518, from the rector of St Martin's
grammar school in Brunswick, Heinrich Hanner. In it he
cautiously sought Müntzer's opinion on the validity of
indulgence-selling, in particular whether papal pro-
nouncements carried greater authority than the Gospel.
Whether Hanner broached the issue before the publication of the *Ninety-Five Theses* or Luther's *Sermon on Indulgence and Grace*, which came out in the spring of 1518 and
had a Low German printing in Brunswick later that year,
remains uncertain.[8] Müntzer's reply, if any, is not
recorded, but we do have some indication of his religious
influence upon members of the circle of lay piety. The
brewer, Hans Hornborch, from a Westphalian family of
merchant drapers, an early adherent of the reforming
movement in Brunswick who was known as a religious
visionary and enthusiast, fell under Müntzer's sway. His
desire to escape the lure of worldly possessions and trust
in God's grace alone is attested by another of Müntzer's
close associates, Hans Pelt:

> [He] does not want to be a merchant and will not
> take anything on apart from his brewery, for he only
> wants enough to live on; he puts his trust in God
> and has no great concern for temporal goods.[9]

Renunciation of creaturely desires as the preparation for
true inner faith was to become the hallmark of Müntzer's
mature theology.

His standing amongst the pious layfolk of Brunswick is
tellingly revealed in a letter from Hans Pelt's servant,
Claus Winkeler, in 1515, in which he addressed Müntzer
as a 'castigator of unrighteousness' and signed off with a
phrase drawn from mystical spiritualism 'in the fiery love
of purity'.[10] Müntzer's influence in these circles continued
even during his absences from the city. Between 1515 and
1516 he found employment as provost and schoolmaster

at a house of canonesses at Frose, near Aschersleben, where he also took in children of his contacts in Brunswick as pupils.[11] The only remaining evidence of his priestly activity in Frose is copies in Müntzer's own hand of two offices of St Cyriacus, the convent's patron saint, whose stylised and repetitive form may have heightened his disquiet at traditional expressions of faith. At all events, there is no doubting that Müntzer had already begun to question Catholic institutions and teachings without recourse to Luther's writings and before he had met the great reformer in Wittenberg.

Only recently has an exact dating been advanced for that encounter. It now appears that Müntzer was in Wittenberg in the autumn of 1517, where he attended lectures on Jerome given at the university in the winter semester by Johannes Rhagius Aesticampianus. That might imply that Müntzer spent as much as eighteen months in Wittenberg, before his next known station in Leipzig in January 1519, though whether he could have supported himself for so long without salaried employment from the residue of his Brunswick chantry seems doubtful, even if he took in private pupils. Unbroken residence in Wittenberg seems improbable, moreover, since Müntzer is known to have paid a brief visit to Rothenburg ob der Tauber in Franconia, early in 1518 or 1519. During the Wittenberg months he was exposed not only to Luther's theology but to the humanist involvement with ancient philosophy and rhetoric as well. From Aesticampianus's lectures Müntzer jotted down details of Plato's life, and was particularly drawn to his emphasis on asceticism, which paralleled Müntzer's own mystical concern with suffering. He was also influenced by Quintilian's great work on rhetoric, the *Institutio oratoria*, and seems to have taken the Latin teacher's concept of a natural order (*ordo rerum*), the relationship of the parts to the whole in both logic and nature, as the framework for his own distinctive doctrine of the 'order of all creatures', a universe in which God and man were originally and mutually conjoined.[12]

Despite these humanist strains in his thought, Müntzer was chiefly concerned to get to know the mainsprings of Wittenberg theology from its exponents at first hand. His familiarity with Luther's critique of the late medieval papacy was certainly demonstrated at Easter 1519 by his sermons in the small town of Jüterbog, north-east of Wittenberg, where he had been invited to stand in for the council preacher, Franz Günther. The two men had met in Wittenberg, and when Günther asked the town council of Jüterbog for leave in the face of angry representations by the local Franciscans, whom he had attacked from the pulpit, it seemed natural to suggest Müntzer, who was then without a salaried post apart from his modest chantry in Brunswick, as his replacement. Müntzer's arrival, however, only made matters worse, for he took up the attack on the Franciscans where Günther had left off. The only evidence for his preaching is contained in a report by one of the friars, Bernhard Dappen. Dappen's testimony has not been regarded as completely reliable: he described Müntzer, for instance, as having been expelled from Brunswick. Whatever the truth of that allegation – probably a hint that Müntzer had offended the city's ecclesiastical hierarchy by anticlerical utterances very much as in Aschersleben a few years earlier – Dappen was at least an eye-witness at Müntzer's sermons in Jüterbog. As such, he provides the first detailed account of Müntzer's early theological and religious concerns.

Dappen lists eleven 'articles' which Müntzer expounded: they fall, in effect, into three categories. He began by upholding the conciliarist principle that the papacy was subordinate to a General Council of the Church, which should be convoked at regular intervals; the popes instead had arrogated to themselves rights,

such as the canonisation of saints, which once had properly belonged to councils. None of the great teachers of
the Church, he went on, the early fathers and the later
saints, upon whom the papacy based its tradition of authority, had ever demonstrably converted a heathen to
Christianity; this tree of knowledge, in other words, could
not, of itself, impart faith. These teachers had relied,
moreover, upon reason to elucidate faith – here Müntzer
was above all challenging the scholastic method of
Aquinas – yet reason derived from the devil. Lastly, he
asserted, the bishops scorned their pastoral duties;
because these tyrants failed to carry out annual visitations
their clergy had become negligent, ignorant and venal.
As a consequence, the Holy Gospel had lain unheeded
for four hundred years.[13]

At first glance, these sentiments are conventional
reformist stuff, straight out of the Wittenberg lecture hall:
no surprise, therefore, to find his Catholic opponents
decrying him as a 'Martinist', an early follower of Luther.
And yet the thrust of Müntzer's critique, especially his
dismissal of the Church fathers, is more than a mere attack
upon Catholic tradition and authority; by implication he
rejects the entire apparatus of theological scholarship as
a path to faith. The experience of true faith must lie
elsewhere.

This crucial question, once broached, would not let him
go, and it was to nag him later that spring on a visit to
Orlamünde, just south of Jena. During his month-long
stay there, very possibly at the invitation of Andreas
Bodenstein von Karlstadt, another radical reforming
figure who was rector of the parish and who had apparently grown close to him at Wittenberg, Müntzer
immersed himself in a study of Johann Tauler, the most
practical of the medieval German mystics, whose doctrine
of the reception of the Holy Spirit in the 'abyss' – the
innermost depths – of the soul as the precondition of

true faith was to become the cornerstone of his mature theology. Although he may well have encountered Tauler and the works of other German mystical writers in Wittenberg (Luther, who had read Tauler's sermons, embraced a theology of the Cross which echoed the mystics' concern with the tribulation of the soul, though his theological interpretation of suffering differed from theirs[14]), Müntzer approached Tauler with intentions quite different from those of Luther. His reading, according to the one extant report, appears to have been inspired by Karlstadt's cook at the Orlamünde rectory, by all accounts a woman of unusual piety and holiness. Müntzer, therefore, was not looking at Tauler through the eyes of a textual scholar and intellectual but rather as a seeker after mystical enlightenment, who appreciated the spiritual wisdom to be found in a simple, unlettered woman.

From Orlamünde he probably travelled to Leipzig in June 1519 to attend the public disputation between the Wittenberg reformers and their Catholic opponents in the hall of the Pleißenburg palace. Ranged against Karlstadt, Luther and Melanchthon in debate was the old Church's most formidable polemicist, Johann Eck, professor of theology at Ingolstadt. Müntzer was no more than a silent spectator at the rounds of theological jousting, but he cannot fail to have digested the essential message of the reforming party: that the Church as it stood, Roman and pontifical, constituted a grave historical deformation of the early Christianity manifest in the Catholic apostolic church. It can be no coincidence that Müntzer straight away set about furiously buying books on the history of the early Church. From a Leipzig bookseller he ordered Eusebius's *Chronicle* in two volumes, with Jerome's additions, the pseudonymous Hegesippus's Latin adaption of Josephus's *Jewish War*, the complete Jerome, and the letters and sermons of Augustine. He must also have bought the ten volumes of Eusebius's *History of the Church*, to which he refers in the *Prague Manifesto*. What confronted him, particularly in the pages of Eusebius, was the image of a virgin church of undimmed vitality and spiritual purity, which had been seduced by a corrupt and arrogant priesthood, thereby ignoring Eusebius's conviction that the Church had been vouchsafed a remarkable restoration through Constantine's conversion in the fourth century.[15] The deformation of the Church, he concluded, had taken place at a very early stage, even as early as the mid-second century. For Müntzer the length of time in which the Gospel had remained unheeded was no longer four hundred, but well over one thousand years.

Müntzer found ample time to study these authors in depth whilst confessor to a house of Cistercian nuns at Beuditz near Weißenfels, halfway between Leipzig and Naumburg, during the months of December 1519 to April 1520. He seems to have been filling in time in this badly paid appointment, since Luther had already recommended him at the Leipzig disputation to Johannes Sylvius Egranus, the humanist preacher of Zwickau who was looking for a suitable deputy to cover for him on a protracted leave of absence. In Beuditz the duties were not onerous and Müntzer, on his own admission, at last enjoyed the leisure to read and reflect on the Church fathers, whilst continuing to explore the German mystics, both Tauler and his contemporary, Heinrich Suso. So far his career had been a rootless series of shifts and starts in temporary or ancillary employment, interspersed with journeys far and wide beyond his native Saxony. He may (very doubtfully) have visited Antwerp through his Brunswick contacts, but he certainly went south to Franconia early in 1518 or 1519, where he stayed in Rothenburg ob der Tauber.[16] Not long afterwards Müntzer was to describe himself as wandering at large in the world to spread the word of God.[17] These itinerant years seem to cast Müntzer as an early Bunyan's Pilgrim, on his journey through life's afflictions to the Shining Gate. It was only with the much delayed departure of Egranus from Zwickau that Müntzer emerged from the shadows to the centre of the Reformation stage. In the first weeks of May 1520 he stepped into Egranus's shoes as preacher of St Mary's, Zwickau. His mature career had at last begun.

Notes

1. At the beginning of the *Prague Manifesto* (1521): 'Ich, Thomas Müntzer, bortig von Stolbergk . . .', F 495.
2. Ulrich Bubenheimer, 'Thomas Müntzer in Braunschweig', part I, *Braunschweigisches Jahrbuch*, LXV (1984), 37–48; part II, ibid., LXVI (1985), 79–114. Here part II, 112.
3. CW 6 f. For the dating of the letter to 25 July 1515, rather than 1517, cf. Ulrich Bubenheimer, 'Thomas Müntzer und der Anfang der Reformation in Braunschweig', *Nederlands Archief voor Kerkgeschiedenis*, LXV (1985), 3.
4. Václav Husa, *Tomáš Müntzer a Čechy* (Rozpravy československé Akademie Věd, Řada společenskych věd, Rŏcník LXVII, Sešit 11) (Prague, 1957), 13.
5. E 20.
6. On Müntzer in Brunswick see Bubenheimer, 'Müntzer in Braunschweig', parts I and II, and 'Anfang der Reformation'.
7. Siegfried Bräuer, 'Thomas Müntzers Beziehungen zur Braunschweiger Frühreformation', *Theologische Literaturzeitung*, CIX (1984), 637.
8. Cf. CW 9–10, n. 23.
9. Ibid. 38.
10. Ibid. 6 f.
11. Manfred Kobuch, 'Thomas Müntzer in Frose', *Zeitschrift für Geschichtswissenschaft*, XXXVII (1989).
12. Ulrich Bubenheimer, 'Luther – Karlstadt – Müntzer: soziale Herkunft und humanistische Bildung. Ausgewählte Aspekte vergleichender Biographie', *Amtsblatt der Evangeli-*

sch-Lutherischen Kirche in Thüringen, xl (1987), 66–7; idem, 'Thomas Müntzers Wittenberger Studienzeit', *Zeitschrift für Kirchengeschichte*, xcix (1988), 178–92; idem (ed.), 'Thomas Müntzers Nachschrift einer Wittenberger Hieronymusvorlesung', ibid., 214–37.

13. CW 447 ff.
14. Cf. Steven E. Ozment, *Homo Spiritualis. A comparative study of the anthropology of Johannes Tauler, Jean Gerson and Martin Luther in the context of their theological thought* (Studies in Medieval and Reformation Thought, VI) (Leiden, 1969).
15. Abraham Friesen, 'The intellectual development of Thomas Müntzer' in Rainer Postel and Franklin Kopitzsch (eds), *Reformation und Revolution. Beiträge zum politischen Wandel und den sozialen Kräften am Beginn der Neuzeit. Rainer Wohlfeil zum 60. Geburtstag* (Wiesbaden, 1988).
16. On Müntzer's journeys see Bubenheimer, 'Müntzer in Braunschweig', part II, 99–102.
17. CW 33.

2

In Zwickau and Prague

Müntzer arrived in Zwickau from the seclusion of Beuditz at the beginning of May 1520. His decision to take up the temporary preachership in the south Saxon industrial centre was clearly deliberate, for he chose it in preference to the offer of a curacy in Elsterberg, a village further to the south-west, which the incumbent, Heinrich von Bünau, was pressing upon him. The prospect of a decent salary can hardly have moved him, for as Egranus's deputy he received an annual stipend of 14½ florins, barely more than his chantry in Brunswick was worth, which he still retained. Rather, he relished the opportunity of honing his exceptional talents as a robust and rousing preacher which had first been revealed in Jüterbog. Unlike the haughty retiring Egranus, who preferred the quiet of his study, Müntzer reached out eagerly to embrace his congregation with impassioned sermons: the pastoral concern for his flock which was to become an abiding hallmark of his ministry in Allstedt is already visible in the Zwickau months.

Zwickau, on the southern borders of electoral Saxony, was a powerhouse of the early capitalist economy in central Germany. Its prosperity had been founded upon a successful textile industry, but by the late fifteenth century the town was beginning to benefit from the boom in iron-ore- and more especially silver-mining in the

Erzgebirge, the rich-seamed mountain range which strad-
dled the frontier with Bohemia. Zwickau, although it had
its own iron-foundries, grew in wealth and size as the
market centre and provisioner of the mining communities
throughout the region, notably Schneeberg, Annaberg,
and Joachimsthal. By the 1520s its population was nearing
7000, having doubled from the fifteenth century, which
made it nearly as large as Leipzig, though nowhere near
the size of Erfurt (with around 18 000 inhabitants) or,
indeed, Brunswick. Such rapid growth could not conceal
that Zwickau's prosperity, which remained too heavily
dependent upon the fluctuating demand for woven cloth,
rested on fragile foundations and brought dire social
consequences in its wake. The old guild framework of
independent mastercraftsmen bent and buckled as the
greater manufacturers and merchants, who invested
heavily in mining enterprises, broke the shackles of regu-
lated competition and employment to amass large
fortunes and bring the lesser masters with puny capital
resources into economic dependence upon them. Within
the clothmakers' guild the strains became particularly
acute.[1]

Müntzer's first sermons continued the attack which he
had launched in Jüterbog upon the Franciscans. He
accused the mendicants of hypocritically soliciting alms
from the anxious faithful, who were led to believe that
salvation was the reward for the outward observance of
Christian precepts. One friar from nearby Weißenfels, in
particular, he denounced for belittling the profundity of
Christ's passion in denying the need for all Christians to
share that Godforsakenness in their innermost selves as
the preparation for true faith. The uproar which followed
these sermons prompted the swift intervention of the
bishop of Naumburg and confronted the Zwickau council
with a difficult choice. Many citizens, in a town with a
long tradition of clandestine heterodox opinion, inclined

to the new religious doctrines, and they were already familiar with Egranus's attack upon the Franciscans' cult of St Anne, to whom a famous altarpiece had been dedicated in the parish church of the mining town of Annaberg. Though the ferocity and commitment of Müntzer's preaching threatened to drag Zwickau into unwanted and dangerous conflicts, the council still gave its unanimous backing to Müntzer against the ecclesiastical hierarchy. This support has rather too readily been equated with acquiescence in Müntzer's religious views. Certainly amongst its members there were devoted followers, including the mayor, Dr Erasmus Stella (or Stuler), but the council as a whole was rather taking a political decision to uphold its right to determine church affairs within the walls, a struggle for autonomy which had late medieval roots in many German cities. Once Egranus returned in the autumn, however, cracks began to appear in the façade of reforming solidarity, as irreconcilable differences of theological understanding between humanist scholar and radical preacher became impossible to ignore.

For his part, Müntzer turned in July to Luther to explain his actions and seek support. His appeal was primarily intended to expose the errors of his adversaries, rather than to expound his own convictions, so that it offers little direct insight into his religious thinking. The letter does in fact show a close affinity with Luther's theology of the Cross, and it was signed 'Thomas Müntzer, whom you brought to birth by the Gospel'. Whether the letter was ever sent remains unclear; no reply from Luther has survived. That Müntzer should regard Luther as his mentor is testimony enough to his reforming orientation in the early Zwickau months, but that need not imply a complete identity of theological intentions. It was, in the end, on the very meaning and purpose of Christ's passion that Müntzer, with his mystical understanding of faith, came to differ most profoundly with the Wittenberg

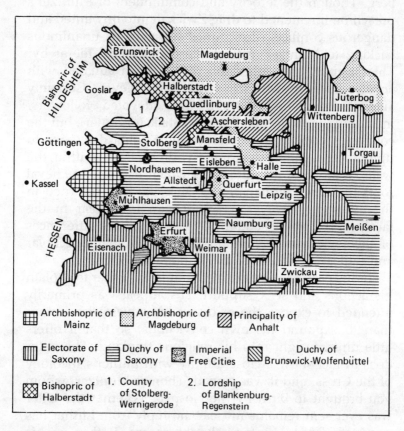

Archbishopric of Mainz

Archbishopric of Magdeburg

Principality of Anhalt

Electorate of Saxony

Duchy of Saxony

Imperial Free Cities

Duchy of Brunswick-Wolfenbüttel

Bishopric of Halberstadt

1. County of Stolberg-Wernigerode

2. Lordship of Blankenburg-Regenstein

MAP 2 Thuringia around 1500

reformer. In any case, one of Müntzer's sermons that September (if correctly reported by the town clerk, Stephan Roth) on the Virgin Mary as mediator between God and man reflected in its dogma and imagery an utterly medieval devotion in the tradition of St Bernard with no overtones of evangelical belief at all. This should make us cautious not only of pigeonholing Müntzer's theology while still half-formed, but also of branding him as a polemical agitator from earliest days.

The Zwickau council cannot have seen in Müntzer a subversive influence, for it was keen to retain his services after Egranus's resumption of his post at St Mary's. A solution was found by appointing Müntzer to another preachership at a different church, St Catherine's, from 1 October 1520. There at last he held a permanent post on full salary, 25 florins per annum. The parish of St Catherine's housed many of Zwickau's clothworkers. With over one hundred masters it was the town's leading guild, but by that token it had also suffered the greatest division of labour and social stratification as a consequence of early capitalist business practices. Alongside the richer masters there were ranged many more poorly paid journeymen clothmakers, hired wage-labourers who made up an early industrial proletariat, gathered into their own fraternity, on whose behalf the masterclothiers had endowed an altar in St Catherine's in 1475. Many of the parishioners seem to have cultivated a form of piety which expressed their socio-economic predicament: it identified suffering – material as well as spiritual – as the precondition of faith, and stressed the mystical illumination of untutored layfolk. Foremost amongst these pious figures was Nikolaus Storch, a masterclothier from an impoverished patrician family and self-taught master of Scripture, who rejected the mediation of the priesthood and believed that God revealed himself in dreams and visions.

Despite the presence of Storch and his associates

Müntzer's new church should not be contrasted too
sharply with the more sedate St Mary's. St Catherine's
was also the castle church of Zwickau, and its parishioners
were by no means all impoverished. Although Müntzer
achieved a lasting rapport with the humbler weavers of
his congregation, his following was never confined to that
group alone or even his own parish; on the contrary,
throughout his stay in Zwickau he kept support amongst
sections of the propertied bourgeoisie, including some
rich clothmerchants.[2] The emergence of rival factions
behind Egranus and Müntzer in the autumn of 1520 does
not betoken, therefore, any simple division within the
community between upholders of the magistrates' right
to reform the Church in Zwickau and advocates amongst
the poor citizens of a more radical and egalitarian
spirituality.

Nevertheless, the gulf between the two preachers was
visibly widening. Müntzer's repeated public attacks on
Egranus for his superficial understanding of religion
reached the point where the humanist requested the
council in December to relieve him of his duties. Even
Luther's close associate, Johann Agricola, who had delivered a friendly warning to Müntzer some weeks earlier to
refrain from taunting the cold and aloof scholar, admitted
that Egranus was theologically illiterate, a view ultimately
shared by Luther himself. The council, however, was
reluctant to let Egranus go until it had found a replacement. It approached both Luther and Müntzer for names,
and the latter suggested Franz Günther, his erstwhile
colleague in Jüterbog. Nothing was to come of these
plans, and Egranus did not finally leave Zwickau until
April 1521, by which time the hostility between the two
men had erupted into a fusillade of satirical abuse in
pamphlets and popular ditties.

Throughout the winter, though, the old religion
remained the chief target of Müntzer's sermons. From the

pulpit on St Stephen's Day 1520 he denounced to his face Nikolaus Hofer, a priest from nearby Marienthal, who had accused him of heresy and had come to spy on his sermons. Thereupon Hofer was ejected from St Catherine's by an angry congregation, pelted with dung and stones in the churchyard, and only escaped with his life by taking to his heels out of town. At first sight this incident seems to confirm the image of Müntzer as a violent and inflammatory agitator so sedulously propagated by his enemies. The Zwickau council does not seem to have thought so, for three days later it agreed to call Hofer to account for his unwarranted accusations of heresy, but left Müntzer entirely unscathed. In fact, such disturbances were part and parcel of the early reforming movement. In many cities crowds, often of youths or students, gathered to attack Catholic parsons in rowdy outbursts of anticlericalism. Such incidents, known collectively as *Pfaffenstürme*, occurred in both Wittenberg and Erfurt between 1520[3] and 1523[4].

Of course, Müntzer was no milk-and-water preacher. 'You breathe nothing but slaughter and blood', Agricola admonished him in the spring of 1521. Yet the first shots of open warfare were fired at Müntzer, not by him. A flysheet containing threats and abuse was pushed through his door in mid-January, after he had demanded the forcible expulsion of Catholic priests. A month later his window-panes were smashed by unknown vandals. How far supporters of the old Church in general, rather than of Egranus himself, were responsible is hard to tell. But in the ensuing volley of defamatory lampoons the supposedly mild and retiring Egranus certainly did not lack popular sympathy. On 10 April 1521 Müntzer himself apparently raised a false alarm of fire in the early hours of the morning. Later he denied all knowledge of any disturbance, though he did concede that some of the weavers were planning to kill the existing councillors; a rumour was also circulating that Müntzer wished to install 'twelve apostles and seventy-two disciples' in their place. Empty threats of this kind were, perhaps, to be expected when social and economic antagonisms were evidently on the increase in Zwickau, but it is less certain what interpretation should be put upon the religious vocabulary. Later that year the council was informed that a secret brotherhood of weavers was in existence – an apparent reference to the 'Zwickau prophets', who had known links with Müntzer.[5] Yet to regard Müntzer as the *spiritus rector* of these activities, a clandestine organiser of opposition to the secular authorities, in a conscious prefigurement of his Christian leagues in Allstedt and the Eternal League of God in Mühlhausen, is to make too much of hindsight.

The likelihood of public disorder if the war of words continued nevertheless gave the town council sufficient pretext to intervene. It had already moved in February to appoint a new town pastor, Nikolaus Hausmann, a known Lutheran, and, once its efforts to restore peace between the two preachers had failed, it decided that they must both leave Zwickau. On 16 April Müntzer was formally dismissed, on the grounds that he had lent his name to a shameless pasquil in which the hapless Egranus was mocked as a bibulous voluptuary who hobnobbed with beautiful ladies and the local bigwigs. On hearing the news, a crowd of weavers, both journeymen and masters, from St Catherine's parish assembled to give Müntzer safe-conduct out of Zwickau. The council, fearing trouble, promptly detained over fifty of them. Though he was later to protest his innocence of these events – he claimed to have been in the bath – he realised that his position was hopeless and chose to flee the town under cover of darkness. The weavers were released the next day.

Nothing in the chain of events surrounding his

dismissal suggests an attempted civic revolution; neither is there any hint in the council's decision that it had come to suspect Müntzer of preaching unacceptably radical religious doctrines: he was exiled because he had broken the public peace. At the same time, his preaching clearly struck a chord with the congregation of St Catherine's, amongst whom were Storch's disciples, a group to whom Luther later dismissively referred as the 'Zwickau prophets'. There is reason to think, therefore, that Müntzer's religious views became less obviously Martinian as he encountered and absorbed the distinctive spirituality of Storch's circle.

This argument finds some support in the 'Propositions of Egranus', a list of theological axioms attributed to Egranus which Müntzer compiled in order to refute the humanist's understanding of Scripture, but which with the sudden departure of both men from Zwickau he never published. To reconstruct Müntzer's thinking by simply standing the 'Propositions' on their head is not without risk, since it assumes that he was concerned to give an objective summary of Egranus's position. Nevertheless, certain strands of thought can be pinned down. Where Egranus declared that the experience of faith was confined to Scripture, and must therefore be interpreted by theologically trained clerics, Müntzer asserted the role of the unlettered but spiritually attuned laity in championing a true understanding of faith against a self-righteous priestly caste. Where Egranus believed that the Holy Spirit had been bestowed upon the apostles alone,[6] Müntzer argued that God's Spirit was eternally at work throughout Creation. Above all, just like the Franciscans, Egranus was accused by Müntzer of playing down the abiding significance of Christ's passion: suffering must daily be relived in the agony of each believer's soul. The mystical emphasis on suffering as the prelude to faith surfaces in Müntzer's notes for a sermon in Zwickau:

Anyone who wants faith must endure the work of
God and not be entangled in creaturely things. . . .
The work of God is as bitter as the abyss of hell. First
unbelief has to get the better of counterfeit faith, and
one has to stand before God quite helplessly. It is
God's doing that he deprives man of all comfort. To
start with, the best thing is to pass one's whole life
under review and suffer enough to balance the
damage done by the lusts of the flesh.[7]

How far Müntzer was nudged towards a mystical stress
on suffering by Storch and his followers has been hotly
debated. Müntzer later kept up correspondence with
several members of the circle, notably Markus Thoma (or
Stübner), a former student of Melanchthon whom he had
got to know in Wittenberg, and who apparently
accompanied him after Zwickau on his next journey that
summer to the Bohemian capital Prague. The link with
Prague has given rise to febrile speculation that the
'Zwickau prophets' maintained close contacts with the
Hussite movement in Bohemia. Zwickau had long-
standing economic and commercial ties with its south-
eastern neighbour, and there is certainly some evidence
that it had been a centre of Waldensian and Taborite (that
is, radical Hussite) heresy during the fifteenth century.
Any lingering influences upon Storch's circle, however,
remain purely hypothetical. When Storch and two close
friends, Markus Thoma and Thomas Drechsel, had an
audience in December at Wittenberg, Melanchthon and
Nikolaus von Amsdorf were at once impressed and bewildered by what they heard. They acknowledged Storch's
extensive biblical knowledge but took exception to his
questioning of infant baptism, his emphasis on direct
personal illumination by God, and his mystical sense of
belonging to God's Elect in the last days of the world.
These doctrines betray no obvious affinity with the Tabor-

ites, except perhaps for the undercurrent of chiliasm, though that was not infrequent amongst lay conventicles in the later Middle Ages. Whatever notions Storch and his associates may subsequently have expounded, they cannot have been the carriers of chiliastic doctrines from the Taborites to Müntzer during his stay in Zwickau.[8] That is not to deny that echoes of Storch's beliefs can be found in Müntzer's thought at the time: he had praised him, after all, in a sermon as more learned in Scripture than any priest. But Storch and his associates were probably adherents of the medieval heresy of the Free Spirit, whereas Müntzer's mystical-spiritualist theology descended in a direct lineage from Tauler. Müntzer's ascetic temperament must have recoiled from the libertinism – especially sexual – which characterised these heretics, and there are signs that Müntzer later came to identify the 'Zwickau prophets' as false brethren for that reason.[9] His self-description in a letter to Nikolaus Hausmann as a 'servant of God's Elect' need not derive from Storch at all: the latter, indeed, may have copied it from Müntzer. Given what we now know about Müntzer's contacts in Brunswick, there is no need to spin an elaborate net of mystical influences in Zwickau: Storch may be as much pupil as master.

Müntzer's susceptibility to mysticism and his respect for the piety of simple layfolk were nothing new – they had been demonstrated during his brief visit to Orlamünde. By the same token, mysticism was only one strand of his maturing theology. Despite the controversy with Egranus, Müntzer's encounter with humanism in Wittenberg made a lasting impression, and he retained the friendship of humanist graduates in years to come. Two book-lists in his possession around this time show how widely he read from current controversies sparked by the Wittenberg reformers back through the humanists, medieval mystics and Church fathers to classical rhetor-

icians and philosophers. By 1521, under the carapace of
Martinianism, Müntzer was beginning to forge these
highly disparate sources and authorities with astonishing
boldness into an independent theology of striking originality. Its first flowering came that autumn in Bohemia
with the composition of the radical appeal to true Christianity in the *Prague Manifesto*.

From Zwickau, Müntzer appears to have made a brief
reconnaissance in the spring over the border to Žatec
(Saaz), a community with old-established Taborite
connections. There he may have been urged to undertake
a longer trip to Bohemia, for on his return to Saxony he
was making hasty arrangements in June 1521 for a journey
to the Bohemian capital, Prague, where he was to stay
until December. The letters he wrote whilst quartered
near Elsterberg, the home of Markus Thoma's father, the
village bathkeeper, give a startling insight into Müntzer's
frame of mind during these summer months. He was
clearly preparing for a protracted sojourn, since he
instructed Thoma on 15 June to join him the very next
day, having seen to the storage of goods and chattels left
to Müntzer by his mother. 'Our undertaking', he urged,
'will brook no delay.' A friend in Jena, Michael Gans, was
asked to look after his papers which, Müntzer added, he
would make over formally to Gans 'should death befall
me'. 'I will journey throughout all the world for the sake
of God's Word', he concluded in a flight of pathos. Likewise, he wrote a curious letter to the new pastor of
Zwickau, Nikolaus Hausmann, chivvying him to nurture
the seed of faith which Müntzer had planted. He had gone
to Bohemia, he said – this is the phrase which implies a
previous visit in the spring – not for love of glory or
money, but rather in the expectation of his imminent
death, lest his preaching of the mystery of the Cross

should perish. Calling himself a servant of God's Elect, he invoked (perhaps only figuratively) the prophet Elijah who had slain the priests of Baal – a theme which recurs in the *Prague Manifesto*.

What can account for the agitated and morbid tone of these letters? The admonition to Hausmann contains a clue. Towards the end Müntzer refers to Matthew ch. 24, v. 14:

And his gospel of the kingdom shall be preached in all the world for a witness unto all nations; and then the end shall come,

and declares, 'The time of Antichrist is upon us'.

How far Müntzer was already in the grip of millenarian expectations of the Last Days is hard to tell; the apocalyptic strains in the *Prague Manifesto*, though certainly present, take second place to the elaboration of a mystical theology, in which the themes of suffering and tribulation, the core of his later beliefs, are first adumbrated. The sense of peril and foreboding evinced in Müntzer's correspondence is confirmed by the fears expressed a month later by one of his close adherents in Zwickau, Hans Sommerschuh. There were rumours that Müntzer had been persecuted or poisoned, that he was gravely ill or even that he was dead. Yet the flurry of apprehension bears no relation to the cordial and ceremonious manner in which he was apparently received in Prague. Our knowledge of his arrival is contained in a letter from one of his Brunswick friends, the merchant Hans Pelt, in September, keeping him abreast of events in that city. The details in both this and a previous letter concerning Müntzer's decision to surrender his chantry in Brunswick make it plain that Pelt still regarded Müntzer as a Martinian. It is likely, therefore, that the warm welcome given to Müntzer was intended to honour a representative of the Wittenberg movement. The discovery that Müntzer was no longer (if he ever had been) Luther's mouthpiece caused these sentiments rapidly to cool.

Despite sombre doubts about his fate, Müntzer was quite clear in his own mind what the purpose of his visit to Prague was. It was not to imbibe pure Taboritism at source, whatever his links with Storch's circle and Markus Thoma might once have suggested, but to preach the true Gospel to the Bohemians. To that end he had tried to persuade a Czech, Hans Löbe, to accompany him, presumably as an interpreter, and only when the latter cried off did he resort to Thoma. The choice of Bohemia was, of course, no accident. The example of Hus a century earlier and the sustained defiance of the papacy by the Czech nation gave Müntzer hope that in Bohemia he might restore Christianity to its original purity through the establishment of a new apostolic church. Luther, too, had after all signalled his approval of the Hussites as pioneers of Christian reform.

By 1521, however, the Hussite movement in Bohemia was in considerable disarray. The utraquists – that is, those who upheld the administration of the sacrament in both kinds, bread and wine – were divided amongst themselves. The moderates, whose assertion of Czech independence had dwindled to little more than a belief in the lay chalice, were being challenged by a new set of radical utraquists eager to reinvigorate the Hussite tradition by returning to its origins. Alongside these groups there existed the quite separate congregation of the Unity of Czech Brethren, which espoused a literal biblicism. Müntzer found himself caught in the mills of sectarian turmoil. His first acquaintance is likely to have been with academics (he was put up to begin with in the Collegium Carolinum attached to the university) and the utraquist clergy; his ignorance of Czech was bound to inhibit close contacts with the citizenry at large, though a rump of Germans remained in the city. Relations with the educated elite of Prague, it appears, quickly became strained, for Müntzer was ejected from his university residence and went instead to stay for three months at the home of a leading citizen, very possibly the recorder, Burian Sobek, a follower of the new utraquists, who had studied in Wittenberg and helped get some of Luther's works published in Prague.

Within days of his arrival – on 23 June – Müntzer had mounted the pulpit. A Czech humanist records hearing Müntzer (whom he described as a 'Lutheran') preach in German that morning in the Corpus Christi chapel, and the same afternoon in Latin at the Bethlehem chapel. Both were university churches (the latter had been Hus's own chapel), and he is also known to have preached and celebrated communion with the help of Czech interpreters in another prominent utraquist church, St Mary's in the Old Town. What Müntzer preached we are not told, but from the continuities between his letter to Hausmann and the drafts of the *Prague Manifesto* it can reasonably be inferred that he attacked the false understanding of faith with which the Catholic clergy seduced its flock. Indeed, his uncompromising and implacable anticlericalism has been seen as the linch-pin of his theological development.[10] His mystical approach to faith which saw the everlasting word of God reach out into men's hearts beyond the dead letter of Scripture led Müntzer to denounce not only clerics of the old faith or humanist intellectuals such as Egranus, but the moderate utraquists, and possibly the Unity of Czech Brethren as well, whose biblical devotion he must have regarded as a hollow sham. Therein must surely lie one cause of the growing estrangement between Müntzer and a populace which so recently had warmly greeted his arrival, and it has been conjectured that the drafting of the *Prague Manifesto* in

November represents a last attempt to retrieve an audience which was slipping from his grasp.

The *Prague Manifesto* (the 'Protestation concerning the situation in Bohemia', in Müntzer's words) has always presented historians and theologians with formidable difficulties of interpretation. It exists in four versions, a shorter and a longer German, a Latin, and a partial Czech translation.[11] None of these was published during Müntzer's lifetime. Of the surviving texts, the shorter German and the Latin are in Müntzer's own hand. Great play has been made of the contrast between the German (especially the longer) and Latin versions, the former bursting with drastic denunciations of a corrupt clergy and larded with apocalyptic imagery, the latter more restrained, studded with biblical references and clearly intended for an educated readership. The milder Latin version, accordingly, has sometimes been seen as a conscious watering-down of the fiery spirit of the German texts, by which Müntzer concealed his true intentions, demagogic and violent, from the authorities in Prague in a cloak of well-turned phrases. To fix upon the contrast in language and style, however, is to miss the real congruities in content between the longer German and Latin versions. The stages of Müntzer's theological-historical argument unfold in similar ways; key concepts and images recur in both texts. It is now in fact generally agreed that the longer German version follows, rather than precedes, the Latin; its coarseness of tone may derive from Müntzer's frustration at the mounting hostility towards him in Prague. That leaves the shorter German version. Because it is dated 1 November, a full three weeks before the longer version of 25 November (the Latin version merely carries the year 1521), it can be taken as the first bald statement of Müntzer's concerns, a skeleton fleshed out in the later texts. What marks it out is its size: it is written on one vast sheet of paper, over a yard square.

That has led some scholars to think that it was indeed intended as a 'manifesto', to be posted on the door of a Prague church, just as Luther's *Ninety-Five Theses* against indulgences were supposedly pinned to the door of the castle church in Wittenberg. This is hard to credit, for who in passing could have read the closely written text, let alone digested it? It is not inconceivable, however, that Müntzer designed it in this singular format as a dummy for a broadsheet placard. Circumstances in Prague made it difficult to find a printer, and after his departure Müntzer may have considered that its explicit appeal to the Czechs ruled out a sympathetic audience in Germany. At all events, the existence of German and Latin versions, and the incomplete Czech translation, indicate that Müntzer was aiming at the widest possible public in Bohemia.

In all its versions the *Prague Manifesto* constitutes a sustained tirade against the clergy. Müntzer arraigns them on two heinous charges: they feign an understanding of faith by exalting the dead letter of Scripture over the living voice of God speaking directly to men's hearts; and they fail their flocks because in their learned arrogance they deny the fear of God which is the beginning of faith. Actively, they know nothing of the order of creation which links God with mankind; passively they experience nothing of the suffering and temptation by which men empty themselves of creaturely desires to receive the full-ness of God's Spirit. These axioms recur in countless vari-ations in the *Manifesto* texts and in his later writings. Müntzer presents not so much a logical argument as a succession of allegories and images which describe and elaborate his central themes.

At the beginning Muntzer declares the mystical character of faith:

But St Paul writes to the Corinthians, in the third

chapter of the second epistle, that the hearts of men are the paper or parchment on which God's finger inscribes his unchangeable will and his eternal wisdom, but not with ink; a writing which any man can read, provided his mind has been opened to it. . . . God has done this for his elect from the very beginning, so that the testimony they are given is not uncertain but an invincible one from the holy spirit which then gives our spirit ample testimony that we are the children of God.[12]

The clergy, by contrast, merely spout the Scriptures without any inner understanding in their hearts:

They are like the stork which gathers up frogs from the fields and the swamps and then disgorges them undigested to its young ones in the nest. That is what the usurious, interest-exacting priests are like, who gulp down the dead words of Scripture and then pour out the mere letter and the untried faith (which is not worth a louse) upon the poor, really poor people. The end-result is that no one is sure of his soul's salvation.[13]

Müntzer demands not a dumb God, which is all that the dead letter of Scripture can offer, but a God whose word is eternal and alive, who speaks directly to man. This notion derives ultimately from Meister Eckhart and Dominican mysticism, though Müntzer probably received it from the *Book of Spiritual Poverty*, wrongly attributed to Tauler. The authentic voice of Tauler is then heard when Müntzer sets the Word against the Spirit. Without the sevenfold receipt of the Spirit, he proclaims, man cannot hear the living word of God – a clear echo of Tauler's seven stages of salvation which included temptation and suffering. For Müntzer these tribulations become the cornerstone of his doctrine of the fear of God. Those who receive the Spirit through tribulation and forsakenness will experience true faith; those who will not empty themselves of creaturely desires remain sinful and cannot experience God. In the contrast between experienced and inexperienced, true and counterfeit faith, Müntzer distinguishes the elect from the damned.[14]

> I affirm and swear this by the living God: anyone who does not hear from the mouth of God the real living word of God, and the distinction between Bible and Babel, is a dead thing and nothing else. But God's word, which courses through heart, brain, skin, hair, bone, marrow, sap, might and strength surely has the right to canter along in quite a different way from the fairy-tales told by our clownish, testicled doctors. Otherwise no one can be saved; otherwise no one can be found. The elect must clash with the damned and his forces must collapse before the latter.[15]

But when the unity between God and man, which has been destroyed by man's fall from grace, is restored, the kingdom of this world will be given to the elect: they shall inherit the earth. Here Müntzer fuses his mystical theology with the humanist categories he had encountered in Wittenberg. Only the eager admission of the Holy Spirit into the depths of the soul can restore the necessary relationship between God and man as a cosmological unity, the 'inner order' innate to God and all his creatures, as a precondition for the transformation of the 'outer order', the structure of worldly society and government.[16] Underpinning this 'order of creation' is Müntzer's abiding biblicism, most evidently his interpretation of the book of Genesis.[17]

What has caused the breakdown of God's natural order?

Müntzer turns for an answer to the early church historians, whose accounts he had begun to read two years earlier.

> This intolerable and noxious canker from which the Christian people suffers has moved me in pity to read the history of the early fathers with all diligence. I find that after the death of the apostles' pupils the immaculate virginal church became a whore by the adultery of the clergy; it was the fault of the scholars, who always want to sit up top, as Hegesippus writes and then, after him, Eusebius in Book 4, chapter xxii.[18]

Since those days the Church has been deformed beyond recall:

> Because the people allowed its right to choose the priests to fall in disuse, from that time on the convening of a proper council proved impossible. If anyone did want one, it was the devil's doing, for what was dealt with in the councils or consultations was mere child's play: bell-ringing, chalices and cowls, lamps and locums, the adoration of masses; as to the real living word of God, not once, not once did they jerk open their jaws, nor did they as much as mention the order (of creation).[19]

The failure of the councils to reform the Church was bound to strike a chord in Bohemia, whose own reformer, John Hus, had been burnt at the stake by the decree of the council of Constance in 1415.

Yet the days of depravity are now numbered. At the end of the longer German version of the *Manifesto* the heat of Müntzer's anger bursts into an apocalyptic flame:

> Such errors had to take place so that all men's deeds,

those of the elect and those of the damned, could
flourish freely until our time when God will separate
the tares from the wheat. . . . O ho, how ripe the
rotten apples are! O ho, how soft the elect have
become! The time of the harvest has come! That is
why he himself has hired me for his harvest. I have
sharpened my sickle, for my thoughts yearn for the
truth and with my lips, skin, hands, hair, soul, body
and life I call down curses on the unbelievers.[20]

Müntzer exhorts his Czech listeners to help purge the
godless priests who have seduced the Church, as Elijah
destroyed the priests of Baal, and declares:

For the new apostolic church will start in your land
and then spread everywhere. I will be prepared so
that when the people in the churches address a question to me in the pulpit I will satisfy every single
person. If I cannot demonstrate such mastery and
knowledge then let me be liable to temporal and
eternal death. There is no greater pledge that I can
offer. Anyone who scorns this warning is already
doomed to fall into the hands of the Turk. After the
wild rage of the latter the real Antichrist will reign
in person, the real opponent of Christ, who will soon
afterwards give the kingdom of this world to his elect
for all time.[21]

What weight to place on the apocalyptic strains in the
Prague Manifesto is not easy to decide, but the temptation
to read backwards from Müntzer's later career must be
resisted. The letter to Hausmann shows clearly Müntzer's
preoccupation with apocalyptic ideas,[22] yet he is neither
a direct follower of Joachim of Fiore nor a simple adherent
of Taborite chiliasm. More important than his denial of
any debt to Joachim (Müntzer claimed to have read only

the tract on Jerome, in any case falsely attributed to Joachim) is Müntzer's emphasis on the universal and exclusive illumination of faith through the Holy Spirit, which is not Joachite at all. Equally, he shares with the Taborites a belief in the millennium,[23] but unlike them insisted that the Last Days of Antichrist had already begun, during which the outward purging of Christendom and the gathering of the elect were to follow an inner purification of the soul through the Spirit. Rather, the apocalyptic of the *Manifesto*'s closing passage provides the historical framework in which Müntzer envisages his mystical theology being fulfilled (a vision which he was to work out three years later in the *Sermon to the Princes*), whilst the concept of a natural order supplies its analytic category.

Müntzer's penchant for drastic and inflammatory language far outruns any apocalyptic intentions, but it gives a telling insight into his mental world. The images of sundering and winnowing, the stark counterpoint of godless and elect, false and true faith, suggest a strongly dualistic mind married to a schismatic temperament, unable or unwilling to prevaricate or compromise. Müntzer was a man of passion whose encompassing solicitude and warmth towards his flock were mirrored by hatred and defamation of his enemies. And, as so often with such men, those whom Müntzer had once admired he came most bitterly to detest.

Something of this divisiveness must lie behind Müntzer's expulsion from Prague that winter. The details are obscure, but Müntzer seems to have alienated the very group upon whom he pinned the greatest hopes. By the beginning of December he was apparently under some form of house arrest and shortly thereafter was summarily ejected. That there were real hostilities is confirmed by the treatment received by his companion, Markus Thoma, who claimed on his return to Saxony to have been stoned by the citizens. Whether theological, political or merely personal antagonisms were to blame is impossible to tell.

After six months in the city, however, the singularity of Müntzer's religious vision cannot have failed to strike all who heard him preach and teach. In fusing the many disparate influences of his early career into a distinctive theology Müntzer in the *Prague Manifesto* cuts the leading traces of Wittenberg. The mystical foundation of his theology, grounded in extensive reading amongst the German mystics and sharpened by his personal contacts in Brunswick and Zwickau, is set in an intellectual framework derived from his humanist study of classical authors and given a historical urgency by his borrowings from apocalypticism. Though Müntzer weaves these strands with great dexterity into a bundle of ideas, loose ends remain; the cast of Müntzer's mind, intuitive, allegorical and visionary, indeed forbids excessive rigour and coherence; a strong anti-intellectual streak emerges in his distrust of the casuistic book-learned and his preference for the inspired unlettered layfolk. 'I do not despair of the people', he declared, in contrast to the stiffnecked and pharisaical priests, who are beyond redemption. But what actions did Müntzer suppose would follow upon his exhortations? How was the new apostolic church in Bohemia to be established? All Müntzer offers his audience in Prague is the threat of dire retribution at the hands of the Turks if his appeal goes unheeded. He had become a prophet without honour in a foreign country.

After Prague Müntzer's track once again becomes lost in a wilderness with few signposts in the sources. In December 1521, perhaps in response to his own prompting, he was invited to teach doctrine in the monastery of St Peter in Erfurt. Whether he was able to take up the offer is not known; the monks' letter had spoken of grave dissensions amongst the fraternity, doubtless precipitated by the new religious doctrines. He may well have stayed that winter in Erfurt, though, for he did not accompany Markus Thoma to the discussion at Wittenberg between the 'Zwickau prophets' and Melanchthon and Amsdorf. Certainly he was in touch with developments there, for at the end of March 1522 he wrote to Melanchthon from Erfurt criticising the turn of events in Wittenberg since Luther's return from protective exile in the fortress of Wartburg earlier that month. Despite friendly assurances at the outset – 'Your theology I embrace with all my heart' – Müntzer showed no compunction in expressing reservations about the basis of Luther's advocacy of clerical marriage and his rejection of purgatory. Luther's purely biblical justification Müntzer regarded as another instance of the dead letter of Scripture: the Wittenbergers were invoking a dumb, not a living, God, and destroying the creative power of the Spirit in men's souls. In eschatological fervour – 'Dear brothers, leave your dallying, the time has come! Do not delay, summer is at the door!' – he upbraided Luther for his forbearance towards the hesitant and weak in faith, insisting that he make no peace with the reprobate. These points of attack reveal the widening theological division between Müntzer and Luther, already implicit in the *Prague Manifesto*. The rejection of scriptural faith as a dead letter, with the Bible at best an exemplar of God's word, at worst a mortifying instrument of divine law, runs counter to Luther's stress on the Gospel as the fountainhead of faith – *sola scriptura*. The chasm between good and evil contradicts Luther's notion of man as both sinner and saved – *simul justus et peccator*.[24] The thrust of Müntzer's anticlericalism, first focused on the Catholic clergy, then directed against such tepid intellectualising humanists as Egranus, was now turned fatefully upon the Wittenberg reformers themselves. He had learnt of the eight Invocavit sermons in March 1522 designed to bring Wittenberg to order after the erratic leadership of Karlstadt, in which Luther preached against indiscipline and commotion in the pursuit of reform. Müntzer suspected him thereby of snaffling the free expression of inspired faith in the name of public peace and the interests of the civil magistrates. 'Do not flatter your princes', he warned, 'otherwise you will live to see your undoing' – a piece of tinder later to ignite the powder-keg of the Peasants' War.

To talk of battlelines in 1522, however, is utterly premature. Müntzer was as much puzzled as enraged by what he saw as backsliding on Luther's part. In the storm years of the Reformation there were no entrenched positions, no established orthodoxy. Luther's cause was still imperilled, his word by no means holy writ. Müntzer had as much right to voice his theological concerns as any other evangelical. Amongst the Saxon reformers Müntzer was indeed a pioneer in cultivating contacts with the world of south German and Swiss theology, from the cautious figure of Oecolampadius in Basel to the Zürich Anabaptist radicals under Conrad Grebel. Nevertheless, he was beginning to encounter persistent hostility from those who called themselves Lutherans. In Erfurt he seems to have fallen foul of the professor of Greek at the university, Johann Lang, one of Luther's closest correspondents, and later that summer he was subjected to abuse from Lutheran supporters in Nordhausen.

These were undoubtedly months of great desolation and uncertainty for Müntzer. Already in January his colleague in Jüterbog, Franz Günther, had enquired anxiously after his whereabouts: the most disturbing rumours were circulating about his fate, and Günther wondered whether Müntzer had not been seized by a false spirit, namely the Devil. After Erfurt Müntzer's itinerary becomes a matter of conjecture. Before Easter he returned briefly to his birthplace Stolberg to deliver a series of apparently well-received sermons. He may then have set off on the first of his visits to south German reformers, for at some stage that year (we do not know where) he met Urbanus Rhegius, the Lutheran scholar who had been expelled from Augsburg at the end of 1521. By July 1522 – one of the few secure dates for that year – Müntzer was writing from Nordhausen to defend himself against the 'scribes, pharisees and hypocrites' who were impugning his integrity. Whether he held some temporary post there is again uncertain; by September, at any rate, he was applying unsuccessfully for a church appointment in Allendorf on the western fringes of Thuringia. The next we hear of him is in late November at Weimar, where he apparently took part in the disputation between Wolfgang Stein, the chaplain and court preacher to duke John of Saxony, elector Frederick's brother, and the local Franciscans concerning the Sacraments. It is striking that Müntzer is not recorded as making any intervention on the issue under debate – sacramental questions, apart from baptism, barely feature in his writings, which is extraordinary for a Protestant theologian – but only as reiterating his emphasis on suffering as the prelude to faith through the Spirit.

Shortly before Christmas 1522 he at last found a post to tide him over the winter, when he was offered a chaplaincy with preaching duties at the Cistercian nunnery of St George's in Glaucha, just outside Halle. The salary was low and the price of shelter high, for Müntzer was obliged to dissemble his reforming convictions in a city dominated by the Moritzburg fortress, the residence of the most powerful prelate in Germany, cardinal Albert of Brandenburg, elector of Mainz, archbishop of Magdeburg, and avid promoter of papal indulgences. In public, Müntzer conducted services according to the Catholic rite, an occasion for much jeering by his Lutheran detractors in years to come. Only once did he court detection, when he clandestinely administered communion in both kinds to a widowed noblewoman, Felicitas von Selmenitz, who had close ties with the convent. Müntzer's exposed and dangerous position makes it most unlikely that he had anything directly to do with the rioting against the monastery of Neuwerk in the city in January 1523, when around four hundred citizens tried to sack the convent. Such disturbances were in any case nothing new. As a city under ecclesiastical control Halle had a rich and varied tradition of anticlerical outbursts in the later Middle Ages. On his own admission, it will be recalled, Müntzer had taken part in agitation against archbishop Ernest of Saxony over a decade earlier.

There is no reason, therefore, to treat Müntzer with kid gloves, but his expulsion from Halle in March need not be attributed to the January disorders. Once his cover was blown, his religious views alone would suffice to secure his dismissal. Yet he must have been able, however precariously, to have amassed some sort of following in Halle, for he sent back words of solace to his supporters in a letter which sums up the months of hardship and tribulation, both physical and mental, in apocalyptic hope:

> No one can experience God's mercy until he has been forsaken. . . . So let my suffering be a model for yours. Let all the tares shoot up as much as they like; they will all have to come under the flail with the pure wheat; the living God is sharpening his sickle in me so that I will later be able to cut down the red poppies and the little blue flowers.[25]

In these months theology and biography – theory and practice, if one will – coincide. Müntzer was experiencing the very desolation which he believed was essential preparation for the bestowal of God's Spirit. That is what gave

44 *Thomas Müntzer*

him his sense of inner strength and righteousness, which
affliction could only stiffen. Yet at the nadir of his fortunes
he was rescued. He found a permanent post as pastor in
the little town of Allstedt, to the west of Halle, possibly
through the influence of his patroness, Felicitas von
Selmenitz, whose father and husband had both been
Saxon officials there. It was in Allstedt that Müntzer, with
the opportunity and security to put his vision to the test,
was at last able to lay the foundations of his religious
revolution.

Notes

1. Susan Karant-Nunn, *Zwickau in transition 1500–1547. The
   Reformation as an agent of change* (Columbus, O., 1986), ch. 3.
2. Cf. Siegfried Bräuer, 'Die zeitgenössischen Dichtungen
   über Thomas Müntzer und den Thüringer Bauernauf-
   stand. Untersuchungen zum Müntzerbild der Zeit-
   genossen in Spottgedichten und Liedern, im Dialog und
   im neulateinischen Epos von 1521 bis 1525' (Diss. theol.
   University of Leipzig, 1973), 31.
3. Cf. Ulrich Bubenheimer, 'Luthers Stellung zum Aufruhr
   in Wittenberg 1520–1522 und die frühreformatorischen
   Wurzeln des landesherrlichen Kirchenregiments', *Zeitschrift der Savigny-Stiftung für Rechtsgeschichte, Kanonistische
   Abteilung*, cii (1985), 161 ff.
4. Cf. R. W. Scribner, 'Civic Unity and the Reformation in
   Erfurt', *Past and Present*, lxvi (1975), 40 f.; reprinted in
   idem, *Popular Culture and Popular Movements in Reformation
   Germany* (London/Ronceverte, W. V. 1987), 196 f.
5. Cf. Siegfried Bräuer, 'Müntzers Feuerruf in Zwickau',
   *Herbergen der Christenheit. Jahrbuch für deutsche Kirchengesch-
   ichte (Beiträge zur deutschen Kirchengeschichte, VIII)*, 1971,
   127, 145.
6. This point is confirmed in Müntzer's letter to Nikolaus
   Hausmann of 15 June 1521. CW 34.
7. Ibid. 387.

8. Siegfried Hoyer, 'Die Zwickauer Storchianer – Vorläufer der Täufer?', *Jahrbuch für Regionalgeschichte*, XIII (1986), 73 f.

9. Cf. Abraham Friesen, 'Thomas Müntzer and the Anabaptists', *Journal of Mennonite Studies*, IV (1986), 146 ff., 150.

10. Hans-Jürgen Goertz, ' "Lebendiges Wort" und "totes Ding". Zum Schriftverständnis Thomas Müntzers im Prager Manifest', *Archiv für Reformationsgeschichte*, LXVII (1976), 164 f.

11. On the correct order of the versions cf. E 188ff. and the introduction by de Boor in Max Steinmetz, Friedrich de Boor and Winfried Trillitzsch (eds), *Thomas Müntzer. Prager Manifest* (Leipzig, 1975).

12. CW 358.

13. Ibid. 367.

14. Goertz, ' "Lebendiges Wort" und "totes Ding" ', 159 ff.

15. CW 368.

16. Hans-Jürgen Goertz, *Innere und Äußere Ordnung in der Theologie Thomas Müntzers* (Studies in the History of Christian Thought, II) (Leiden, 1967).

17. Cf. Rolf Dismer, 'Geschichte – Glaube – Revolution. Zur Schriftauslegung Thomas Müntzers' (Diss. theol. University of Hamburg, 1974), 7ff. On this question cf. also Gottfried Seebaß, 'Müntzers Erbe. Werk, Leben und Theologie des Hans Hut' (Theologische Habilitationsschrift University of Erlangen, 1972).

18. CW 360.

19. Ibid. 370.

20. Ibid. 370–1.

21. Ibid. 371.

22. Cf. Richard Bailey, 'The sixteenth century's apocalyptic heritage and Thomas Müntzer', *Mennonite Quarterly Review*, LVII (1983), 34.

23. Cf. Reinhard Schwarz, *Die apokalyptische Theologie Thomas Müntzers und die Taboriten* (Beiträge zur historischen Theologie, LV) (Tübingen, 1977).

24. Cf. Goertz, ' "Lebendiges Wort" und "totes Ding" ', 172.

25. CW 54.

3

Ministry in Allstedt

The market town of Allstedt, situated thirty miles to the
south-west of Halle in northern Thuringia, was a territorial enclave of the Saxon electors, surrounded by ducal
Saxon lands and the sovereign counties of Mansfeld and
Querfurt, the latter belonging to the secular territory of
archbishops of Magdeburg. As part of the Thuringian
possessions of the ernestine branch of the Saxon house
of Wettin, the district of Allstedt was ruled by the elector's
brother, duke John, who resided in Weimar, and was
administered from Allstedt castle by his local tax-official,
Hans Zeiß. The success of Müntzer's ministry in Allstedt
from April 1523 to his ultimate dismissal in August 1524,
the longest sojourn in his short and storm-tossed life,
turned upon the town's peculiar political situation. The
benign tolerance which elector Frederick extended to the
Wittenberg reformers, and duke John's genuine religious
concern, initially ensured that Müntzer, too, was safe
from immediate interference in the ernestine enclave. In
the long run, however, that success bred its own failure,
for the rapid and enthusiastic response to Müntzer's
preaching from countrydwellers in the neighbouring territories provoked alarm among their rulers, who were
without exception staunch Catholics and who had set
their face resolutely against any manifestation of heretical
beliefs.

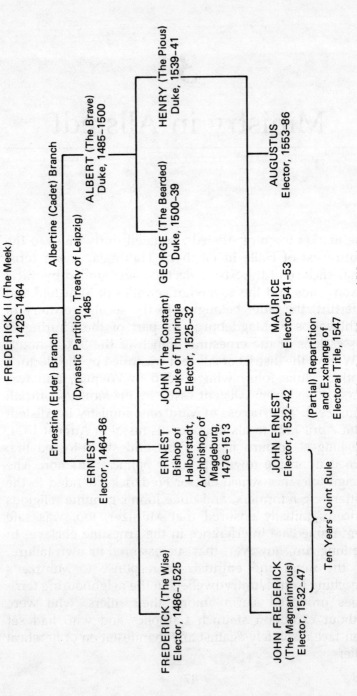

FIGURE 3 The Saxon House of Wettin

FREDERICK II (The Meek)
1428–1464

Ernestine (Elder) Branch

(Dynastic Partition, Treaty of Leipzig)
1485

Albertine (Cadet) Branch

ERNEST
Elector, 1464–86

ALBERT (The Brave)
Duke, 1485–1500

FREDERICK (The Wise)
Elector, 1486–1525

ERNEST
Bishop of
Halberstadt,
Archbishop of
Magdeburg,
1476–1513

JOHN (The Constant)
Duke of Thuringia
Elector, 1525–32

GEORGE (The Bearded)
Duke, 1500–39

HENRY (The Pious)
Duke, 1539–41

JOHN FREDERICK
(The Magnanimous)
Elector, 1532–47

JOHN ERNEST
Elector, 1532–42

(Partial) Repartition
and Exchange of
Electoral Title, 1547

MAURICE
Elector, 1541–53

AUGUSTUS
Elector, 1553–86

Ten Years' Joint Rule

At the outset it was far from obvious that Allstedt would provide fertile soil for radical religious doctrines. The small community, numbering perhaps six hundred in all, displayed few signs of the social and economic ferment which had convulsed Zwickau; nonetheless, the town contained perceptible distinctions of wealth and status, not least between the craftsmen (among them two immigrant goldsmiths) and the bulk of peasant burghers with close ties to the countryside.[1] Moreover, whilst there were no ecclesiastical foundations to provide a target for anticlerical resentments in Allstedt itself, the town lay in a district teeming with convents, twenty within a radius of ten miles, many of which were in sharp decline on the eve of the Reformation. Two of the nearby convents, Naundorf and Walkenried, had property and rights in the town. Of the two churches in the Old and New Towns (rather highfalutin designations for what was little more than a village), the abbey of Walkenried held the advowson of St Wigberti's in the Old Town, whose incumbent, Simon Haferitz, embraced the new doctrines and quickly became a loyal lieutenant of Müntzer, whilst the right of presentation to St John's in the New Town lay with the elector himself, who in fact never officially confirmed, whether by oversight or act of policy, the town council's decision to install Müntzer as pastor.

Against this unpromising background Müntzer had succeeded within weeks of his arrival in attracting large crowds to his services in St John's. A later report that on Sundays up to two thousand people flocked to his sermons from the surrounding countryside is by no means improbable, given that in both its churches Allstedt offered the only evangelical worship for miles around. But the sudden attraction of Allstedt clearly derived above all from Müntzer's personal impact. In his sermons Müntzer may have expounded his unique vision of faith, but it was chiefly through his recasting of the traditional

forms of church service that he was able to win the hearts
and minds of his swelling congregation. Müntzer's
liturgical reforms, which are central to any understanding
of his spiritual and pastoral concerns, are by any stan-
dards an extraordinary achievement, yet they have been
strangely overlooked by generations of historians.[2] The
sounding brass of confessional polemics has deafened
scholars to the originality and warmth of Müntzer's evangelical services, as he sought to lead his flock by prayer,
hymn and sacrament gently but steadfastly to the true
experience of Christ.

Müntzer's liturgy comprised two main devotional
works and an apologia. In the *German Church Service*, a
prayer-book for the offices of the church year, Müntzer
placed before his congregation the first full liturgy in the
German language. It simplified and reduced the Catholic
offices to Matins-Lauds and Vespers alone, with five sets
for the main festivals of the Christian year, Advent, Christmas, Passion, Easter and Pentecost. He used a similar
pattern in his *German Evangelical Mass*, in which conse-
cration of the host was stripped of its Catholic connotations in the act of transubstantiation and redefined as
the mystery of God entering man's soul and filling it
with his Spirit, so that the believer became conformed to
Christ. Müntzer did not hesitate to draw upon existing
missals, especially the Halberstadt Breviary, and he used
Luther's translations of the Psalms where available, and
many ancient church hymns. Throughout, his services
retain much of the form of Catholic worship, with anti-
phons, responsories and versicles. His purpose was not
to destroy traditional forms of worship but to purge them
of what he saw as superstition and corruption, and to
make them accessible to ordinary folk in the vernacular.
By emphasising the active participation of the congregation in daily worship – the joyful singing of psalms and
hymns, the conscious uttering of prayers and responses

– rather than by the passive study of the Bible alone Müntzer believed that the hesitant might be reassured and the doubting receive guidance in the way of faith. For that reason also, Müntzer made his services entirely choral; indeed, he went further by retaining the Gregorian plainsong of medieval Catholic worship. Through the singing of simple and familiar tunes the unlettered would become more receptive to God's Spirit than through formal study of the Scriptures.

The apparent conservatism of Müntzer's liturgical reforms has not only caused modern scholars to underestimate their significance; it also spread dismay amongst his contemporaries. Conrad Grebel, the leader of the Zürich Anabaptists, was to take Müntzer to task in September 1524 for having composed a choral Mass, for which, he maintained, there was no justification in Scripture. Worse than the strictures of a wooden biblicist, however, were the taunts that Müntzer was readmitting popish practices by the back door. Against these charges he drew up an apologia at the end of 1523, the *Order and Explanation of the German Church Service . . . at Allstedt*, in which he explained more fully his liturgical intentions and gave a summary of his sacramental theology. He pointed with justice to the manifold variations in liturgy and rites which had grown up amongst widely scattered Christian communities in Croatia, Armenia, Russia, or amongst the Mozarabs in Spain.

> Why should we not do the same when circumstances permit it? For we are German people in Allstedt, not Italians, and want to burrow our way through the great confusion and find out what it is that we should believe . . . O! What blind, ignorant men we are to vaunt ourselves as the only Christians in outward ostentation, quarrelling madly among ourselves more like beasts than men! Surely every servant of

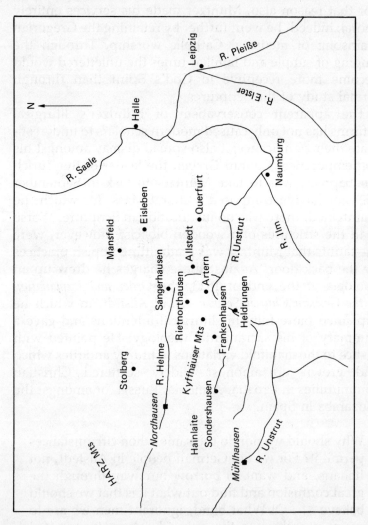

MAP 4 Allstedt and Environs

the word of God has the authority to teach the people
of his parish a pattern of worship using psalms and
songs of praise from the Bible readings to edify
them?[3]

It is entirely in this spirit that Müntzer concedes that
his liturgies may be altered or adapted in the light of
circumstances: they shall not also become a 'dead letter'.
Müntzer appended some brief remarks on the Sacraments, though he never spelt out at any length which he
regarded as the indispensable core of evangelical
theology. He speaks primarily of baptism and the
Eucharist, and in that respect accords essentially with
Luther. His views on infant baptism (which he expounds
more fully in a later Allstedt tract, the *Protestation or Proposition*) have attracted particular attention, inasmuch as
the Anabaptist tradition has variously invoked Müntzer's
name as the father of its beliefs. From the *Order and Explanation*, however, it is clear the Müntzer, whilst expressing
doubts about the efficacy of infant baptism in imparting
God's Spirit in full measure, retained this sacrament as a
provisional ceremony, since he regarded man's whole life
on earth as a baptism of suffering before salvation in the
everlasting life of heaven.
    Despite their outward form, Müntzer's liturgical exper-
iments contain more that is startlingly new than meets
the eye. In the *German Church Service*, in particular, he
shows a surprisingly free hand in his rendering of the
Psalms, going well beyond what either the Vulgate or
Luther's translations warrant, in order to convey his
soteriological concern with suffering and tribulation. In
Psalm 140, to take a striking instance, where his language
is frequently more charged than that of his sources, he
reworks certain verses in a way which unmistakably
reflects his mystical-apocalyptic vision.

King James Bible	*Müntzer*
1. Deliver me, O Lord, from the evil man; preserve me from the violent man;	O God, preserve me from the godless; protect me from the wicked and deceitful:
2. Which imagine mischiefs in their heart; continually are they gathered together for war.	They have sought always in their hearts to pursue villainy; to that end they have filled their days with strife.
3. They have sharpened their tongues like a serpent; adder's poison is under their lips. Selah.	They have sharpened their tongues with poison like serpents. Which dart around like adders' tongues.
4. Keep me, O Lord, from the hands of the wicked; preserve me from the violent man; who have purposed to overthrow my goings.	O Lord, preserve me from the power of the godless and keep me from him full of wickedness, for they seek utterly to destroy my path.
5. The proud have hid a snare for me, and cords; they have spread a net by the wayside; they have set gins for me. Selah.	The evil men have designs upon me, for they seek to trap me with their nets as the birds upon the way.
6. I said unto the Lord, Thou art my God; hear the voice of my supplications, O Lord.	I said unto the Lord: Thou art my God; o Lord, harken to the voice of my pitiful beseeching.
7. O God the Lord , the strength of my	O God, Thou hast protected my head in

salvation, thou hast covered my head in the day of battle.

the insurmountable struggle, that my salvation is not forfeited.

8. Grant not, O Lord, the desires of the wicked; further not his wicked device; lest they exalt themselves. Selah.

O God, let the godless no longer hold sway, for their misdeeds are a hindrance to the entire world, wherein they have exalted themselves in dignity before others.

9. As for the head of those that compass me about, let the mischief of their own lips cover them.

Whenever I sit with them at table, I must devour their godless ways on a plate.

10. Let burning coals fall upon them; let them be cast into the fire; into deep pits that they rise not up again.

O God, give them the tribulation of faith, test them like red gold with coals of fire, so that they fall into a pit from which no one can save them.

11. Let not an evil speaker be established in the earth; evil shall hunt the violent man to overthrow him.

Whoever has not undergone temptation may babble of God as much as he likes, but will discover his downfall.

12. I know that the Lord will maintain the cause of the afflicted, and the right of the poor.

God furthers the cause of the needy and provides for the justice of the poor.

13. Surely the righteous shall give thanks unto

The elect directly seek God's name; the righ-

thy name; the upright   teous blanch not at his
shall   dwell   in   thy   countenance.[4]
presence.

Müntzer's overriding concern to minister to the needs of
the common folk is revealed in his decision to set the
Magnificat at the end of the office for the Passion. The
verses from St Luke's Gospel, 'He hath put down the
mighty from their seats, and exalted them of low degree.
He hath filled the hungry with good things; and the rich
he hath sent empty away' must not be pressed to bear
any consciously rebellious intentions on Müntzer's part,
yet they foreshadow his growing faith in the humble and
meek as the true recipients of God's grace. He had encountered such beliefs before amongst the 'Zwickau
prophets', but they came to exercise him even more as
the progress of his Reformation in Allstedt called forth
the opposition of the secular princes.

Müntzer must have devoted himself to the reform of
worship even before his arrival in Allstedt, for the
liturgical changes were introduced at a pace which
suggests substantial preparation. Their printing,
however, took much longer. It was an extraordinarily
costly and time-consuming venture, which stretched into
late 1524.[5] The undated *German Church Service* is unlikely
to have been published before the autumn and possibly
not until the spring 1524. The *Order and Explanation* came
out at New Year 1524, whilst the *German Mass* did not
finally appear until August that year, with a subsidy from
the Allstedt town council. Müntzer composed a second
foreword to the *Mass*, published separately afterwards, in
which he discussed charges, emanating, it seems, from
Wittenberg, that the Mass was little more than Catholic
mutton dressed as vernacular lamb. The protracted
history of this printing venture underscores the earnest-
ness with which Müntzer approached his ministry in

Allstedt. If it is wrong to think of him trying to establish a 'counter-Wittenberg' in Allstedt, there is no doubt that during these months Müntzer came nearer to realising his vision of a purified community of God's elect than at any other stage in his career.

The early months in Allstedt saw Müntzer at full stretch; he described his exhaustion after a hard day in graphic terms: 'Dealing with people these days means the sort of work which a mother has when her children have dirtied themselves!'[6] But the success of his pastoral ministry brought its own fulfilment. So must likewise his decision, seemingly taken at short notice in June 1523, to marry an unfrocked nun of noble birth, Ottilie von Gersen, who bore him a son the following Easter. About Müntzer's marriage we know next to nothing, but that there was genuine warmth and affection is movingly conveyed in Müntzer's concern for his family's welfare, both after his flight from Allstedt and in his 'recantation' of May 1525.

Although he had at last found a haven in Allstedt, Müntzer was naggingly aware that the Lutherans, who had the ear of the elector and his court, viewed him with mistrust. Luther himself tried to persuade the Saxon official in Allstedt, Hans Zeiß, in late July 1523 that he should urge Müntzer to attend a private disputation in Wittenberg, but the latter refused, sensing that he was being lured into a trap. Instead, Müntzer had already written to Luther in early July, seeking to explain his actions and to justify his theological views in terms amenable to the Wittenberg reformer. In a strange mixture of conciliation and defiance he made no pretence of concealing his attachment to visions and portents rather than biblicism, but insisted that everything he preached and wrote was contained in, and could be verified by, biblical passages. That was, of course, true at a superficial level, but it could not disguise how far apart the two men had grown in their understanding of the Bible as a source of faith. What Müntzer was content to play down in his letter to Luther was spelt out a week later in his warning to the citizens of his home town, a tract which was subsequently published as his first printed work under the title *An Open Letter to his Dear Brothers in Stolberg . . . to Shun Unjustifiable Rebellion*. In language steeped in the mystical tradition, he exhorted the 'elect friends of God' utterly to embrace 'poverty of the spirit', a purging of all creaturely desires and comforts. Only then will God cast down the tyrants from their seats,[7] whose raging is his punishment for the elect's lack of true faith. They must experience the bitter side of faith, believe against belief, hope against hope, before the Spirit can enter men's hearts. In a metaphor which runs throughout his writings, Müntzer likens the afflictions of this world to raging waters:

> But before one can be sure of salvation torrents of water come again and again with thundering so fearsome that one loses the will to live; for the waves of this wild, surging ocean swallow up many who think they have already won through. So one should not flee these waves but negotiate them skilfully, as wise helmsmen do; for the Lord only gives his holy testimony to someone who has first made his way through perplexity.[8]

The tenor of Müntzer's warning leaves no doubt that the Stolbergers must not confuse God's work with rebellion in the name of the Gospel. It is God, not man, who, in his own time, shall destroy the tyrants. The kingdom of the elect must first await the complete renunciation of human desires. Within Müntzer's apocalyptic reading of history, however, it is clear that though rebellion is yet '*unfüglich*' (inappropriate, unrighteous, illegitimate), there will come a time – and those Last Days are upon us – when the elect will and must rise in righteous retaliation (*fügliche Empörung*) against the godless.[9]

However much the godless tyrants might be a manifestation of divine retribution, Müntzer was not willing to tolerate the suppression of the Gospel in the neighbouring Catholic territories. Throughout the summer count Ernst von Mansfeld had used the imperial mandate of March that year to weed out reforming doctrines in his lands north of Allstedt, and had backed it up with a territorial edict of his own. What enraged Müntzer was that the provisions of the imperial mandate, which expressly enjoined all preachers to expound the true Gospel according to the teachings of the Church and to disavow rebellion, could, he believed, be interpreted with equal justice as sanctioning the pure, unadulterated evangelism of the reformers. By mid-September Müntzer was driven to deliver a stinging rebuke to Mansfeld from the pulpit, in which he challenged the count to come to Allstedt with the diocesan bishops and demonstrate in public what was heretical in his teachings. Naturally, Mansfeld was not prepared to stand to account before a preacher who declared 'I am as much a servant of God as you', and who threatened 'If you drive me to the printers [that is, a public denunciation in print], I will deal with you a thousand times more drastically than Luther with the Pope'. In dudgeon, Mansfeld turned to elector Frederick to take action against his unruly subjects in Allstedt, but the wise old ruler merely resorted to the Fabian tactics which had once shielded Luther, and fobbed off the count with vague promises to investigate the matter. Indeed, in his directions to the Allstedt council Frederick assured them that they might keep their pastor provided that he instruct his flock according to Christian principles and not cause annoyance to others.

On 4 October Müntzer composed his own self-defence to the elector which went well beyond a mere rebuttal of Mansfeld's accusations. The letter offers a telling insight into Müntzer's self-perception as a man of God and his attitude towards worldly authority. Casting himself in the role of a prophet come to deliver the 'poor, wretched, pitiable Christian people', Müntzer declared that there can be no mercy shown to God's enemies who oppose the Gospel. If human commandments are allowed to stand in the way of the Gospel, the people will be led astray, 'who should love princes rather than fear them'.

> Princes hold no terrors for the pious. But should that change, then the sword will be taken from them and given to the people who burn with zeal so that the godless can be defeated, Daniel 7.[10]

With that, Müntzer laid bare the contingent nature of worldly rule, a theme he was to elaborate the following summer in his apocalyptic *Sermon to the Princes*. But for the moment Müntzer still trusted in the righteousness of the elector, whom he requested to grant him a hearing 'under divine law'.

Although Frederick did not respond directly to Müntzer's request, the course of events makes it plain that the Saxon authorities intended to keep matters in Allstedt under close scrutiny. In early November 1523 the elector, together with his court preacher, Georg Spalatin, and other officials, spent a week in Allstedt castle on their way to the imperial diet in Nuremberg. The two town preachers, Müntzer and Haferitz, were apparently summoned to a disputation (more likely an interrogation) which was conducted by Johann Lang and two associates specially brought from Erfurt. Spalatin (who was also present) subsequently submitted eleven – very well-targeted – questions on the nature of faith to Müntzer in writing. Although we have no protocol of the proceedings and no copy of the reply to Spalatin, Müntzer's defence can be inferred from two short tracts which were printed around New Year 1524, the *Protestation or Proposition* and *On Counterfeit Faith*.

The *Protestation* (in the sense of a public testimony to the Gospel) contains twenty-two sections which deal with issues of faith. The last four items are clearly postscripts, which may indicate that Müntzer was reworking debating-points which had served him in the castle disputation.[11] Echoing his letter to Frederick the *Protestation* concludes with a request that Müntzer be interrogated 'with my opponents before men of all nations and all faiths', in effect an appeal to world opinion designed to take the wind out of Luther's sails, who was still pressing for a private confrontation in Wittenberg. Little of substance in the *Protestation* is new; the themes are already foreshadowed in the *Prague Manifesto*. Rather more soberly, though, Müntzer now sets forth the contrast between true and false faith. The beginning of faith is the fear of God. Only through the bitterness of godforsaken desolation can the soul be purged of creaturely desires and made ready to embrace the Spirit in its innermost depths. Man's own efforts to acquire faith are doomed to fail; only in resignation and acquiescence (the mystical *Gelassenheit*) can men receive the miracle of faith from God. On this very point Müntzer at last openly turns the scorn which he had hitherto reserved for the Catholic clergy and humanist intellectuals with full force upon Luther. 'The mark is missed completely if one preaches that faith and not works has to justify us.' Justification by faith alone, the cornerstone of all Protestant belief, is for Müntzer a delusion. Man cannot of and in himself claim to have faith: 'man comes to faith solely through the mystical workings of God', not through the 'honey-sweet Christ' whose resurrection brings the promise of redemp-

tion but through the 'bitter Christ' of Gethsemane and
the Cross to whom we must become conformed, in the
'heart-felt groaning and yearning to follow God's will'
which 'is the one infallible mark of true apostolic Christianity'. Nor can faith be found in the pages of the Bible,
as Luther would have it:

> Your biblical scholars say: 'We know that Scripture
> is right.' The truth is that its rightness is there to kill
> you, not to make you alive, for it is not set on earth
> for that. Rather it is written for us ignorant people,
> so that the holy faith, the mustard seed, should taste
> as bitter as if there were no Scripture at all, bringing
> about a tremendous, irresistible feeling of
> consternation.[12]

For other creeds – Turks, Muslims, Jews – too have their
holy books in which they place unquestioning faith. The
Christian Church has been grievously harmed by the
generations of learned biblicists who present faith as a
closed book which only they can unlock. They are in thrall
to their intellectual conceit; they peddle a counterfeit faith
which knows nothing of the poverty of the Spirit; they
cannot explain how true faith is achieved. To drive home
his message, Müntzer attacks the Church's traditional
practice of infant baptism. True faith, he insists, cannot
be bestowed by the external act of sprinkling an innocent
and inexperienced child. Only the bitter experiences of
adult life – despair, madness, error, crime, sin and unbelief[13] – can prepare man for the inward reception of the
Holy Spirit. The biblical scholars have perverted and
distorted the meaning of baptism: 'I would be obliged if
any of our learned men of letters could show me a single
instance from the holy letters [Scripture] where an imma-
ture little child was baptised by Christ or his apostles.'

On Counterfeit Faith, whose printing was held up by

Müntzer's urge to add a welter of biblical glosses, is a more compressed and breathless work than the *Protestation*, saturated with metaphors and highly charged language. Müntzer intended it as an exposition of Matthew ch. 16, but its fourteen sections in fact cover all the points of faith which Spalatin had raised in his eleven questions, though it is too densely and allusively written to be the original answer which he submitted. Many of the themes are adumbrated in the *Protestation*, but now Müntzer addressed himself directly to how the elect may be made conformable to Christ. Faith comes hard: 'none of the fathers – the patriarchs, prophets, the apostles least of all – came to faith without great difficulty.' Müntzer cites the example of the disciples at Emmaus. 'For the depths of their unbelief had to be tested. Not one of them would believe that Christ was risen when it happened.' False understanding of faith, concerned with externals, the flesh not the spirit, has led to sects and schisms amongst Christians.

> If our wretched, crude Christian people is to be saved from such grievous abominations, the first, and all-important, step is to listen to an earnest preacher who, like John the baptiser, will cry out piteously and dolefully in the waste places of the mad, raging hearts of men, so that through God's work they may find the way to become receptive to God's word.[14]

But that preacher – Müntzer! – must beware.

> Sheep are poisoned by bad pasture, but nourished by salt. To preach a sweet Christ to the fleshly world is the most potent poison that has been given to the dear sheep of Christ from the very beginning. For a man who accepts this wants to be God-formed, but

has not the least desire, indeed is totally disinclined, to become Christ-formed.[15]

'Anyone who rejects the bitter Christ will gorge himself to death on honey.'

No one can believe in Christ until he has first conformed himself to him. Through experiencing unbelief the elect leaves behind him all the counterfeit faith he has learnt, heard or read from Scripture; for he sees that an outward testimony cannot create inward reality.[16]

In a final passage, steeped in spirituality, Müntzer declares:

This, then, is the faith which becomes as small as a mustard-seed. Then man must see how he is to endure the work of God, in order that he may grow from day to day in the knowledge of God. Then man will be taught by God alone, person to person, and not by any created being.[17]

These tracts can have left the Saxon authorities in no doubt about exactly where Müntzer stood. It is all the more significant, therefore, that they took no action whatsoever to muzzle him. At Epiphany 1524, Simon Haferitz for his part also preached against the ungodly oppressors of true faith in a sermon which was soon afterwards published. In a passing visit to Allstedt castle in late February, duke John made no moves to intervene with the Allstedt council, possibly because Luther himself was on the verge of sending one of his closest associates, Justus Jonas, to prosecute the differences of religious opinion with Müntzer and Haferitz.[18] Luther's agitation behind the scenes to have Müntzer brought to book availed nothing, for to pious princes of the stamp of duke John the iniquity of Müntzer's doctrines was not – or not yet – apparent. Only when the practical manifestation of those doctrines had politically embarrassing consequences did the attitude of the Saxon authorities begin to change.

Close by Allstedt stood the small chapel of Mallerbach owned by the Cistercian abbey of Naundorf, a shrine whose miraculous image of the Virgin had made it a famous place of pilgrimage. The previous summer, to judge from casual remarks made by Müntzer to Karlstadt, the nuns had been 'stripped of their wealth', which has been taken to mean that the Allstedters were refusing to pay tithes to the nunnery and using the revenues instead to establish a poor chest in the town. By the spring of 1524, however, action against the convent spilled over into violence. One night a small group knocked up the hermit who looked after the chapel and told him to make himself scarce. He refused, and sought advice first from the Allstedt council, which encouraged him to stay put, and then from the nunnery itself, which ordered him to leave, taking the valuable cultic objects with him. The chapel then stood empty. But on Maundy Thursday, 24 March, it went up in flames in an attack of arson which Müntzer himself witnessed. In his confession Müntzer acknowledged that he had preached against the cult of the Virgin as abominable idolatry; he even admitted having seen men from Allstedt carry images out of the chapel and then set fire to it. This statement, however, does not accord with the very detailed testimony of the hermit custodian, who had no reason to absolve Müntzer from responsibility for the attack. If it is doubtful, there-fore, whether Müntzer was directly implicated, there can be no denying that he encouraged iconoclasm, witnessed the arson, and afterwards in no way dissociated himself

from the criminal act. In that sense he was as guilty as
the perpetrators.

The Saxon official, Hans Zeiß, hastily tried to placate the
abbess of Naundorf, but without success. In the strongest
terms she protested to the elector, demanding that the
suspects be tracked down and punished. The first reaction
of the Allstedt magistrates to the attack was to assert
strongly that it was the work of outsiders: in any case,
the abbess was guilty of suppressing the Gospel. Such a
reply could scarcely satisfy the Saxon authorities. On 9
May the council was accordingly summoned to Weimar,
to be told by duke John that he expected action within a
fortnight.[19] Visibly shaken, the councillors on their return
questioned each citizen in turn, but could only find two
men who confessed to any part in the Mallerbach incident. The council's investigations were certainly not aided
by the attitude of the town's two preachers, who on
successive days delivered drastic sermons slighting their
Saxon overlords. Müntzer, it was reported, had called
elector Frederick an 'old greybeard with as much wisdom
in his head as I have in my backside', though he
subsequently denied having uttered the words. Rather
more pointedly, Haferitz declared that 'our princes are
those very people who endowed these convents and churches, which are nothing but brothels and murder-pits'.

Even more awkward was the position of Zeiß himself,
who as the local official had signally failed to round up
any culprits. Under pressure to get results Zeiß, with the
grudging assent of the council, on 11 June arrested one
of its members, Ziliax Knaut, on vague suspicion of
complicity and imprisoned him in Allstedt castle.[20] That
this was an act of desperation is shown by the fact that
Knaut was released without charge a week later, but by
his arbitrary action Zeiß had unwittingly transformed the
political situation within Allstedt. The council clearly felt
itself under direct threat, for on 13 June it drafted an

emergency defence ordinance to enable it to muster the citizenry at short notice. The measure was not intended as a piece of deliberate defiance – a copy was sent to duke John – but it drew a panicky response from Zeiß himself, who ordered the entire council to present itself forthwith at the castle. But before it could accept, the commons intervened to prevent the councillors' attending on the grounds that the summons contravened the new defence ordinance. The council was trapped. It tried to wriggle off the hook by promising to attend the next morning accompanied by members of the commons – a sure sign that the latter distrusted the council's resolve when put on the spot. In the end only the magistrate, Nickel Rucker, was prepared to answer the summons, and he told Zeiß that there was now no hope at all of making any further arrests – events had overtaken the council. Tuesday 14 June was indeed a day of high drama in Allstedt, with Müntzer cast in the leading role. First, a deputation of miners from the nearby Mansfeld territories turned up to lend support to Müntzer and the citizens in upholding the Gospel against its enemies. Though the council hastened to assure Zeiß that it had declined their offer with thanks, the latter was so rattled by the enveloping unrest that he decided to call up reinforcements from the surrounding villages. Nothing could have been more calculated to inflame an already combustible atmosphere. When Zeiß sent a messenger to summon the council once again that evening, the alarm bells were sounded – apparently by Müntzer himself – and the whole town rallied to arms under the defence ordinance. Throughout the night the citizenry remained on the alert, with Müntzer and Haferitz urging them passionately to close ranks in an alliance against the godless. Even the women were told to arm themselves with pitchforks and stand to the town's defences.[21]

In these events Müntzer was clearly acting upon his

apocalyptic belief, already set forth in the *Prague Manifesto*, that the struggle between the elect and the godless in the Last Days of the world was about to begin. Whether a league of the elect was formed in the course of the June disturbances, however, remains very doubtful. From the apologia addressed jointly by council and commons to duke John on 14 June, which clearly betrays Müntzer's hand, he still trusted in the princes to fulfil their divine duty and punish evil, as enjoined upon them by Romans ch. 13, v. 3: 'for we know by the testimony of the holy apostle that the sword has been given to Your Grace to carry out retribution on the evil-doers and the godless and to honour and protect the pious'. There is nothing in the letter to suggest that the sword should yet pass to the common people, as Müntzer had threatened to the elector the previous October. On the contrary, the tone is one of necessary suffering and sacrifice:

> But that we should continue to allow the devil at Mallerbach to be adored, so that our brothers are surrendered to be sacrifices to him, is as intolerable to us as subjection to the Turks. If this leads to force being used against us then the world, and especially the pious elect of God, will surely know why we are suffering and that we are becoming conformed to Christ Jesus.[22]

These seemingly humble sentiments cut no ice with elector Frederick, to whom the letter had been passed on by his brother. In a stern injunction at the end of the month Frederick declared that the evil which the Allsted-ters had combined to destroy by force would be swept aside by God's power and grace alone. In this dictum we can hear the voice of Luther, who had denounced Müntzer to prince John Frederick in mid-June as 'that Satan in Allstedt', and was shortly to publish his famous

Letter to the Princes of Saxony concerning the Rebellious Spirit. Yet before Luther finally succeeded in closing the princes' minds to the doctrines of his acknowledged radical adversary, Müntzer received an unexpected opportunity to expound his theological vision to the Saxon princes in person. It was a chance which he seized with both hands.

At the beginning of July, duke John, his son, prince John Frederick, and their entourage passed through Allstedt on their way to Halberstadt. On the return journey to Weimar they stayed the night of 12 July in Allstedt castle. That evening or the following morning Müntzer was permitted to preach before the princes, either in the castle's small chapel or its parlour, with the chancellor, Gregor Brück, some other court officials, and the local official, Hans Zeiß, in attendance. The unusual circumstances surrounding the sermon have been taken to suggest that Müntzer was formally invited to preach, even that he was being given a belated opportunity to deliver his 'trial sermon' as pastor of St John's, whose advowson was held by the Saxon elector. Had the sermon been commissioned, there would surely have been some record in the official Saxon papers. That, strikingly, there is none makes it much more likely that Müntzer had insisted upon a hearing – if not before the whole world, then at least before the secular overlords in whose hands his fate lay. Within a week Müntzer had revised and expanded the sermon for publication: that it was published at all (and widely distributed) is all the more remarkable, given that Brück and another official had accosted Müntzer on the elector's instructions during their stay in Allstedt castle with the order to submit any tracts from the Allstedt printing press to official censorship.[23]

Müntzer took as his text the second chapter of the book of Daniel, the most famous passage of visionary prophecy in the Old Testament, in which Daniel expounds Nebuchadnezzar's dream to foretell the downfall of all earthly kingdoms and the coming reign of God supreme. Müntzer could not have chosen a text more neatly tailored to both his apocalyptic understanding of history and to his attitude towards religious revelation. In its published form the *Interpretation of the Second Chapter of Daniel* contains a long interlude on the significance and exposition of dreams, the only occasion on which Müntzer addresses in print the nature of visionary theology; whether he could have indulged in such a substantial digression in the delivered sermon, however, seems improbable. The exposition of Daniel ch. 2 offers a rare insight into Müntzer's method of biblical exegesis. He rejected a literal interpretation of phrases and passages from Scripture, insisting instead that chapters be read in their entirety in order to derive their true meaning. Often he collated highly disparate texts in what amounted to free association. With such characteristic boldness Müntzer refashioned Nebuchadnezzar's vision of the four empires of the earth into a new apocalyptic of his own devising whose fifth and final age was dawning.

The *Sermon to the Princes* (as it is commonly known) takes up at the outset a theme first broached in the *Prague Manifesto*, the deformation of the Church. Citing Hegesippus and Eusebius, Müntzer declares that the Virgin Church became a whore after the death of the apostles' pupils. The sectarian dissension which then ensued is mirrored in the Church of his own day, as 'men will also rise up in your midst, who will teach perverse ideas in order to get the disciples to follow them'. These false prophets who have 'robbed the sheep of Christ of the true voice' are as arrogant as the proud biblical scholars who once despised the lowly Jesus in the manger. In their intellectual conceit they teach that 'God no longer reveals his divine mysteries to his dear friends through genuine visions or direct words', and pour scorn on those who claim to have had revelation. With that, Müntzer lumps

all the 'scripturalists' together, Catholic and Lutheran
alike, who know nothing of God's inspiration. Yet he
concedes that the interpretation of visions is no easy
matter. The world has often been led astray by false
interpreters, so that Nebuchadnezzar's caution was altogether justified: 'First tell me what my dream was, and
then give me the interpretation. Otherwise all I will get
from you is deception and lies.' Those who have no
experience of the coming of the Holy Spirit cannot tell
whether dreams are from God or the devil. In Isaiah it is
written:

'What no eye has seen, no ear heard, and no human
heart contained, has been prepared by God for those
who love him. But God has revealed it to us through
his spirit, for the spirit searches all things, even the
depths of the godhead etc.' Hence our earnest
teaching is, in brief, that we need knowledge – not
just some windy faith – so that we can discern what
has come to us from God, from the devil, or from
nature. For if our natural reason is to be taken captive
and made subject to faith . . ., then it must be
brought to the very limits of its own judgement. . . .
But without God's revelation no man can make any
judgement which he can justify before his
conscience. Thus it will become abundantly clear to
him that his cleverness will not help him to traverse
heaven, but that he must first become, in his inward
being, a complete fool. . . . For the more our nature
reaches after God the more the operation of the holy
spirit recedes. . . . [24]

At first sight, Müntzer's attack on natural reason seems
to echo Luther's contempt for reason as the 'devil's
whore', but Müntzer does not believe that the Bible alone
can impart faith. Nevertheless, he is perfectly aware of

the pitfalls of a subjective spiritualism. How are the elect
to know which visions or dreams are of God, or of nature,
or of the devil? Here Müntzer returns not merely to the
necessary purification of the soul through abnegation and
suffering, but roundly declares that the elect must ensure
that 'those figurative images found in dreams and visions
have their parallels in every respect in the holy Bible'. Just
as the Bible is an exemplar (not a conduit) of faith, so also
is it a touchstone of authentic revelation. Genuine visions
are sent by God when man is wracked by greatest tribulation: Jacob's dream of the ladder stretching up to heaven
when fleeing from his brother Esau, and afterwards his
wrestling with the angel; the dream of Joseph in an Egyp-
tian prison; or St Paul afraid to preach to the Corinthians
until reassured by God – Müntzer parades a catalogue
of instances from both Old and New Testaments. Their
authenticity can be measured, Müntzer argues, by the
very reluctance of those visited to believe initially in God's
signs. But in the Last Days God will 'pour out his spirit
over all flesh; and our sons and daughters will prophesy
and have dreams and visions' in abundance.

Müntzer's invocation of visionary prophecy leads him
straight back to Daniel's interpretation of king Nebuchadnezzar's dream of the great image:

> This text of Daniel, then, is as clear as the bright sun,
> and the work of ending the fifth Empire of the world
> is now in full swing. The first Empire is explained
> by the golden knob [the head of the image] – that
> was the Babylonian – the second by the silver breast-
> plate and arm-piece – that was the Empire of the
> Medes and Persians. The third was the Greek
> Empire, resonant with human cleverness, indicated
> by the bronze; the fourth the Roman Empire, an
> Empire won by the sword, an Empire ruled by force.
> But the fifth is the one we see before us, which is

also of iron and would like to use force, but is
patched with dung (as anyone can see if they want
to), that is, with the vain schemings of hypocrisy,
which swarms and slithers over the face of the whole
earth . . . What a pretty spectacle we have before
us now – all the eels and snakes coupling together
immorally in one great heap! The priests and all the
evil clerics are the snakes, as John, who baptised
Jesus, called them, Matthew 3, and the secular lords
and rulers are the eels, symbolised by the fishes in
Leviticus 11. Thus the kingdoms of the devil have
smeared themselves with clay. O, my dear lords,
what a fine sight it will be when the Lord whirls his
rod of iron among the old pots, Psalm 2. Therefore,
my dearest, most revered rulers, learn true judgement from the mouth of God himself. Do not let
yourselves be seduced by your hypocritical priests
into a restraint based on counterfeit clemency and
kindness.[25]

Despite the extraordinary imagery of coupling eels and
snakes, Müntzer is not advocating that the clergy have
no truck with the secular authorities. Rather, he is
warning them of false comforters, those who misread the
signs of the times to preach inaction when the struggle
between godless and godly is being joined. Just as the
Chaldean priests were unable to expound Nebuchadnezzar's dream, so the clergy today default in their duty.

For the condition of the holy people of Christ has
become so pitiable that up to now not even the most
eloquent tongue could do it justice. Therefore a new
Daniel must arise and expound your dreams to you,
as Moses teaches in Deuteronomy 20, he must be in
the vanguard, leading the way. He must bring about

a reconciliation between the wrath of the princes and the rage of the people.[26]

Once the princes recognise the treachery of the false priests they will bitterly regret their benevolence and indulgence towards them. The message is plain. Müntzer, cast as the new Daniel, exhorts the princes to wield the sword against the godless, as Christ says in Matthew ch. 10, 'I am not come to send peace, but the sword'. He is scathing about the 'hackneyed posturings' of those who believe that the power of God will achieve everything without recourse to the sword – a direct riposte to the elector's warning a fortnight before. In executing their divinely appointed task even the princes cannot escape without risk:

> As Psalm 17 says, God is your shield, and will train you for the battle against his enemies. He will make your arm quick to strike and will keep you from harm, too. But at the same time you will have to endure a heavy cross and a time of trial, so that the fear of God may be manifest in you. That cannot happen without suffering, but what will it cost you? Only the risks taken for the sake of God and the vain gossip of your adversaries.[27]

In specifying the princes' target Müntzer recalls God's command through Moses to his chosen people:

> 'You are a holy people. You should show no mercy to the idolatrous. Break down their altars! Destroy and burn their images, if you want to escape my wrath!' Deuteronomy 7. These words have not been superseded by Christ, but he wants to help us to put them into effect, Matthew 5.[28]

Despite therefore his overt estrangement, both personal and theological, from Luther, Müntzer's venom is essentially directed at Catholic practices and superstitions. The Mallerbach incident clearly remains uppermost in his mind. Whatever baleful influence he may attribute to Luther, Müntzer still regards the electoral Saxon princes as godly; indeed, to ensure that the elimination of the godless 'proceeds in a fair and orderly manner, our revered fathers, the princes, who with us confess Christ, should carry it out' by virtue of their office. 'But if they do not carry it out', he warns, 'the sword will be taken from them.' The godless, Müntzer concludes, have no right to live except by the sufferance of the elect, but at harvest-time the tares must at last be rooted out of God's vineyard so that the golden wheat may thrive: 'the angels who sharpen their sickles for the harvest are the earnest servants of God who execute the zealous wisdom of God.'

The deliberate parallel between Nebuchadnezzar and the Chaldean priests on the one hand, and the Saxon princes and Luther on the other, which Müntzer sustains with skill and coherence, can scarcely have been lost upon his exclusive audience, though no immediate reaction to the sermon survives. Above all else, the *Sermon to the Princes* is a treatise on Christian rulership, which may usefully be compared with Luther's earlier tract *Secular Authority: To What Extent It Should Be Obeyed*. Luther assigns the princes an essentially negative, or restraining, role: to preserve peace and public order in a sinful world. To them obedience at all times and unquestioningly is due, for the alternatives – rebellion, sedition, anarchy and war – are too terrible to contemplate. Müntzer, by contrast, enjoins upon the princes a positive duty, that of promoting the Gospel and true faith, both by upholding evangelical preaching and by destroying opponents of the Gospel. Princely power is at once more extensive yet more contingent than for Luther, for those rulers who fail to discharge their Christian office shall be deposed. In his thinking Müntzer seems much closer to the South German and Swiss reformers, notably Huldrych Zwingli in Zürich, who recognised the qualified nature of Christian magistracy and a limited right of resistance to tyrannous rulers in his *Sixty-Seven Axioms*. What distinguishes Müntzer from Zwingli, and from a more irenic figure such as the Strasbourg reformer, Martin Bucer, in particular, is his commitment to an apocalyptic reading of history, which consigns the godless tyrants to perdition in a violent struggle at the end of time. Forms of civil disobedience are quite alien to Müntzer's vision: he is concerned with the fear of God, not the fear of man.

If Müntzer hoped that decisive action against persecutors of the Gospel would follow upon his fervent appeal, he was to be disappointed. Instead, perhaps as a direct consequence of his *Sermon*, Müntzer was summoned to Weimar to give an account of himself at the end of July. In his heart he must have known that the unique opportunity to sway the Saxon princes to his side had come too late. Indeed, in mid-July there is clear evidence that Müntzer was already preparing to take matters into his own hands. Around the time of his *Sermon to the Princes* he urged Karlstadt and his congregation in Orlamünde, together with the nearby villages around Schneeberg, to join a league against the godless. Karlstadt retorted with great heat that 'leagues of this kind are altogether contrary to the divine will', and stated 'quite plainly that I can have no dealings with you about that sort of undertaking or league'. The Orlamünders themselves apparently regarded Müntzer's appeal as an open call to arms, explicitly rejecting his interpretation of the covenant between God and king Josiah in 2 Kings ch. 23, which, they declared, was not an alliance by Josiah with God and

the people but one between the king and his people with
God.

> For if Josiah had bound himself to God and to the
> people too, his heart would have been divided,
> inclined both to God's will and that of men, although
> Christ declares, 'No one can serve two masters.'
> Hence, dear brothers, if we were to ally ourselves to
> you we would no longer be free Christians, but
> bound to men. . . . Then the tyrants would dance
> with joy and declare: These men put their trust in
> the one God, but they ally with one another; their
> God is not strong enough to fight for them.[29]

However much the Orlamünders, clearly prompted by
Karlstadt, may have misunderstood Müntzer's intentions,
their reproach exposed a crucial ambivalence in his understanding of the function and legitimation of such a league.
Was it the work of God or of man? Were its motives to
be defensive or aggressive? Should it embrace both
godless and godly, or solely the elect? To these questions
Müntzer was to give changing and conflicting answers in
the months ahead.

The immediate spur to these confederate plans lay in
the mounting persecution of Müntzer's followers by Catholic lords in the neighbourhood. Friedrich von Witzleben
had attacked peasants in Heygendorf by Allstedt on their
way to hear Müntzer preach, and shortly thereafter had
launched a further bloody attack upon his own villagers
in Schönwerda. In Sangerhausen, on albertine Saxon territory, where the local pastor, Thilo Banse, was a committed
supporter of Müntzer, the local official, Melchior von
Kutzleben, had arrested adherents of the new doctrines
on duke George's instructions. Daily, refugees from the
surrounding countryside poured into the ernestine
enclave of Allstedt to seek protection and support against

their Catholic overlords. In this highly volatile situation Müntzer despatched several letters in quick succession to Sangerhausen, urging the God-fearing to stand fast in the face of affliction and the magistrates to refrain from harassing his colleague Thilo Banse. In doing so he reassured his followers that 'more than thirty leagues and covenants of the elect have been formed', though he made no suggestion that they should join a league there and then. To what these thirty leagues may refer has never satisfactorily been explained; if Müntzer had in mind the conspiratorial groups of his youth in Halle or Asch-ersleben, then those certainly cannot be classed as leagues of the elect under a new covenant between God and man. In any case, his recent efforts to encourage Orlamünde and other communities to join a league against the godless had been brushed aside. Perhaps Müntzer was simply holding out the prospect of speedy deliverance, for he could hardly have concluded a formal alliance with the magistrates of Sangerhausen, who were abetting the suppression of the Gospel. Under renewed threats of imprisonment by Melchior von Kutzleben, Müntzer wrote a third, much longer letter to the 'persecuted Christians' of Sangerhausen around 20 July, in which he left no doubt that they must fear God, not man, even to the point of losing all their worldly possessions:

For the beginning of the wisdom of God is the fear of God. . . . So you should sigh for God day and night with your whole heart, crying out and beseeching him to teach you to fear God alone. For if you do not have this pure fear of God you will not be able to withstand any trial. If, however, you do have it then you will gain victory over every tyrant and they will be so utterly confounded that no words can describe it. The fear of God, however, teaches us that a pious man should be ready to resign himself

completely to God's will, ready to venture his body,
goods, house and home, children and womenfolk,
father and mother, and the whole world too for the
sake of God.[30]

Müntzer then spelt out what the duty of a Christian
towards his prince should be.

A prince and sovereign lord is put there to have
authority over temporal goods, and his power
extends no further than that. . . . Hence you should
speak up boldly and say . . . 'If our lord the prince
has not enough income from dues and rents which
we give him each year then let him take all our goods
as well. . . . But he shall have no authority at all over
our souls, for in such matters one has to be more
obedient to God than to men. . . . If you make us
suffer on this account, we will denounce this and let
the whole world know . . . why we are suffering.
. . . What more can we do?'[31]

To compel Christians to act against their conscience,
therefore, was repugnant, and they must be willing to
suffer imprisonment and punishment for their faith, but
in all other matters they must obey their rulers. A casual
reading of this passage suggests a close affinity with
Luther's dictum that 'suffering, suffering is the Christian's
right, that and no other'. But that would be to overlook
Müntzer's apocalyptic. 'Let the tyrants have their pleasure
with you for a little while, for this unbelieving world has
not deserved any better lords and princes. So let them
plague you as long as God permits and until you come
to recognise your guilt.' The tyrants are indeed God's
punishment upon a sinful world, but their raging is itself
a sign of the Last Days, in which good and evil are locked
in mortal combat. 'For I tell you in truth that the time has

come when a bloodbath will befall this obstinate world
because of its unbelief.' Müntzer holds no brief whatever
for the godless princes:

> How much longer will you go on with false expec-
> tations? Precious little can be expected of the princes.
> So anyone who wants to fight the Turks does not
> need to go far afield; the Turk is in our midst. But
> deal with him as I have indicated above, act so that
> the guilt and the blame are theirs and not yours.[32]

If the Christians suffer harm at the hands of their princes
God will carry out his vengeance at the appointed time.

Whilst Müntzer had not yet given up hope that the
electoral princes and officials for their part would at last
abandon benign inertia for active extirpation of the
godless, he became alarmed at rumours that the Sangerhausen refugees in Allstedt were to be handed over on
request to the Catholic authorities. In great agitation he
wrote to Zeiß on 22 July, demanding to know who had
issued these instructions and pleading with him not to
comply.

> You cannot go turning a blind eye to the other terri-
> tories, as has been customary. For it has become clear
> as day that they have absolutely no time at all for
> the Christian faith. As a result their power is at an
> end and will shortly be handed over to the common
> people.[33]

These threats, it must be stressed, are quite specifically
directed against the Catholic opponents of the Gospel,
such as Friedrich von Witzleben, who

> has broken the common peace and become the very
> epitome of a tyrant and the cause of the whole

rebellion. If he is not punished by the other lords for this then the common peace will completely collapse. For from now on no people will trust their own lord. . . .[34]

They are not directed against secular authority as such. Indeed, in a more emollient mood Müntzer reassured Zeiß later the same day that 'the last thing I wanted was to heap on the pious administrators the fury of the common people'. What had happened, he explained,

> went like this: when Hans Reichart came down from meeting you at the castle he put on an incredibly sad face and reported to them [the refugees] the nature of the warning; they took it to mean that they were to be handed over, and so they came to me and asked if this was our gospel; to sacrifice people on the butcher's block. I was completely taken aback and wondered what had given rise to a question like that. . . . Soon after that I met Hans Reichart coming out of the printer's.[35] Then I said to him: 'What sort of tomfoolery will result if we agree to hand the people over like this?' Then he said you had given him the orders. Then I said, if the administrator at Sangerhausen or any other tyrants came here they should not think that their old tricks would be tolerated here since they had publicly set out to abolish the Christian faith, but that they would be throttled like mad dogs.[36]

Pressed upon all sides and aware of the likely dereliction of his overlords Müntzer in extremity saw the only salvation for his cause in the forging of a new covenant between God and man. In a sermon preached on 24 July Müntzer set before his congregation the example of king Josiah in 2 Kings ch. 23, who led his people to the temple to swear an everlasting covenant with God to keep his commandments, and forthwith ordered the high priest Hilkiah to smite the idolatrous priests of Baal and to destroy their cult. A solemn league and covenant, Müntzer declared to Zeiß, would bind together a Christian people yet 'ill-prepared to shed its blood for the sake of the faith' with their irresolute princes 'while the people still trusts them'. The princes 'must turn their pagan duty and oath to their people into a genuine covenant based on the divine will, so that their people may see with their own eyes that they are taking action'. Only when faced with that solidarity and common purpose will 'the count-less hordes of the godless . . . be pitiably affrighted'.

Müntzer was at pains to make utterly clear to his audi-ence what the nature, scope and purpose of such a covenant should be. As he told Zeiß, it 'will bind together the common man with the pious administrators, solely for the sake of the gospel'. If trouble-makers tried to use it for debased ends, they should themselves be handed over to the tyrants. In particular, he warned that the 'strangers', that is, those from beyond Allstedt's jurisdic-tion in the surrounding Catholic territories, must not be encouraged to think that by joining the covenant they were absolved from rendering dues to their tyrants.[37] The covenant was to be temporary and limited, the work of man, not of God, comprising both elect and damned.

No one should put his trust in the covenant, for he who puts his hopes in man is accursed of God, Jeremiah 17. It should only be a deterrent to the godless, to make them cease their raging until the elect have been able to search the depths of God's knowledge and wisdom with all the testimony pertaining to them. When the pious make a covenant, even though there be evil-doers in it too, the latter will not succeed in pushing through their evil aims.[38]

Above all else, 'the covenant is nothing more than an emergency act of self-defence, something which is admitted by the natural judgement of all rational men'. To those who claim that baptism is covenant enough Müntzer scornfully retorted that true knowledge of God can only be acquired on a long and hard road. 'It is no easy thing to believe and be martyred.' The elect must not sacrifice themselves for a counterfeit goodness and faith. The last thing Müntzer promised of his covenant was ready deliverance or assured salvation.

With Müntzer's words ringing in their ears many of his congregation from near and far streamed after church to the town hall, where they enlisted in a Christian league to defend the Gospel against Catholic attack. Over five hundred men and women were inscribed that Sunday by Hans Reichart, Müntzer's associate and by then one of the town's mayors. They included, it appears, the entire council of Allstedt itself, as well as a large contingent of miners from the Mansfeld lands. The foundation of the Christian league marks the culmination of Müntzer's career in Allstedt, his passage from pastor and liturgical reformer to committed religious activist. Yet most interpretations of the league are shot through with inconsistencies and contradictions.

For many years it was argued that Müntzer formed three leagues in Allstedt: a small conspiratorial association around the time of the Mallerbach affair; a new league of the elect during the June disturbances; and finally the broad defensive covenant of July in the wake of his *Sermon to the Princes*. The sources are admittedly partial and obscure, but recent scholarship has revealed a clearer picture. The testimonies of two league members, Jörg Senff and Claus Rautenzweig, arrested after the peasants'

defeat the following May, confirm that two leagues were
in fact constituted during Müntzer's residence in Allstedt,
but in neither case is a date given. The first comprised no
more than thirty members who were apparently drafted
in secret one lunchtime outside the city gates, pledged to
defend the Gospel and to withhold rents and tithes from
monks and nuns, who should be driven out and
destroyed. It may well be that this league had its origins
in the agitation against the abbey of Naundorf in the
summer of 1523.[39] In its size and purpose it more closely
resembles the anticlerical conspiracies of Müntzer's youth
than the covenanted league of the following year, though
both were sworn in by Hans Reichart, and there was some
overlap of membership. Whatever its activity may have
been in the early months of 1524, there is no evidence
that it was behind the June agitation, or that it was recon-
stituted during those days as a league of the elect. Indeed,
Müntzer's actions between June and July speak strongly
against it. His various appeals to form a league – within
Allstedt itself during the all-night vigil, the letter to
Karlstadt and his followers, his exhortation to the Saxon
princes – all suggest that a broad alliance had not yet been
established. Moreover, if such a covenant had already
been sworn in it is hard to see why the Saxon authorities
did not learn of it until the end of July.

By all accounts, the second league was a public and
official event. Its inauguration took place at the town hall,
and several members subsequently testified that the town
magistrate, Nickel Rucker, and the councillors had
formally enjoined them in Müntzer's presence to swear
on oath to defend the Gospel.[40] This somewhat theatrical
scenario cannot possibly fit the June disturbances, in
which council and commons were at loggerheads. It only
makes sense in the context of the mounting unrest in
the surrounding countryside, the flood of refugees into
Allstedt, and Müntzer's impassioned sermon on 24 July.

Nevertheless, the league's foundation was attended by considerable commotion. In his sermon Müntzer had apparently called the citizens and foreigners to arms. This was taken as an excuse for rowdy street demonstrations, in which the women formed their own contingent and tried to have the church bells sounded in alarm. Uttering threats to withdraw allegiance from their lords and officials – contrary to Müntzer's express injunction! – they vowed to wreak bloody vengeance in the same manner as Friedrich von Witzleben.[41] The heightened sense of fear and foreboding in Allstedt, manifested in these wild outbursts, explains the rush to join the league on the first Sunday, but the ultimate size of the league remains unknown. At first, recruitment seems to have encompassed primarily the Mansfeld miners and the Sangerhausen refugees, including their reforming preacher, Thilo Banse, as well as Müntzer's own following in Allstedt; three hundred of those who joined were described as outsiders. There is, in fact, some indication that the call for a league of mutual defence came as much from the refugees themselves as from Müntzer.[42]

The formation of a Christian league and covenant in Allstedt in July 1524[43] marks a decisive turning-point in Müntzer's career, for it constitutes the essential hinge or clasp between his theological vision and his commitment to social action. Central to his religious concerns was the thoroughgoing purification and renewal of a defiled and deformed Christendom: that reformation would come to pass by means of a new covenant between God and his 'elect friends', foreshadowed in the introductory prayer to his *German Evangelical Mass*.

O gentle Father God I confess to you and your tender son Jesus Christ that I, as a miserable sinner, have acted all my life contrary to your will. . . . Therefore I beseech you elect friends of God presently foregath-

ered to intercede on my behalf with all your hearts,
spirit and might that the mystery of God's covenant
may be revealed through my speaking and your
listening.[44]

In taking on the sins of the world Christ renewed God's
covenant with man:

This is the cup of my blood, the new and everlasting
covenant, a mystery of faith, which is shed for you
and for many for the remission of sins.[45]

For Müntzer, his congregation was not simply a liturgical
entity: he conceived of its acting as one body as well, in a
covenant of the God-fearing. And just as his congregation
embraced both true believers and others weak or hesitant
in faith, so initially his league could not be a covenanted
band of the elect alone. It encompassed righteous and
unenlightened sympathisers alike, wheat and tares. That
accords with Müntzer's wider theological horizons, for at
the outset he regarded the elect not as a small band of
saints but, in principle, as the whole community of Christ,
Christendom at large barring its leading spiritual and
temporal princes. Müntzer's definition of the elect
changed considerably over time – the Bohemian nation,
the ernestine princes, some or all members of his league,
latterly the common people at large – so that he never
worked out a satisfactory theology of predestination. The
explanation surely lies in Müntzer's belief that, in the
sundering of the Last Days, the elect were to be under-
stood not simply as those who possessed true faith but
also as those misled, perverted or oppressed into unbelief,
in other words, the victims of the godless. Equally,
Müntzer's definition of the godless changed over the
years. From the *Prague Manifesto* onwards, where he had
identified the damned with the Catholic church and

clergy, Müntzer gradually widened the category of those he called, from the *German Church Service* onwards, the godless, to include secular rulers who oppressed the Gospel, and, once the Saxon princes had ignored his exhortations, latterly all rulers by virtue of their daily oppression of the common people, whose misery prevented them from achieving true faith.[46] It was at that point that Müntzer's theology finally spilled over into secular rebellion.

The league of July 1524, whatever its avowed intentions, marks the first step down the road which led to his involvement in the Peasants' War. By its foundation Müntzer signalled that he was willing to take matters into his own hands. If the princes would not heed the advice of their new Daniel, then Müntzer had no compunction in compelling them and their officials to act by locking them into an indissoluble alliance with the common people in a league no longer based on civil obligations and allegiance but on a new religious covenant with God.[47] Against that background it is no surprise that Hans Zeiß was himself obliged – seemingly under protest – to join the league.[48] For Müntzer the league was both a preparation for and an instrument of the apocalyptic transformation of the world, by which all worldly sovereignty would pass to God's elect before the kingdom of God on earth. His followers, however, do not seem to have drawn any practical consequences from that vision. Despite the precept contained in Müntzer's confession that all goods should be held in common, leading members of the league in Allstedt continued to buy and sell property. Even the provision that recalcitrants be expelled was never actually enforced.[49]

To the Saxon princes, by contrast, Müntzer's vision must have seemed bewildering. His demand, no less, that their sovereign authority be utterly recast flew in the face of political reality. Quite apart from Luther's admonitions, elector Frederick and his brother John had to take account of the strained relations with their cousin George, the Catholic ruler of albertine Saxony. Their territories lay intermingled; some, indeed, were administered as a condominium. It was quite impossible for the ernestine princes blithely to ignore the repercussions of what would have amounted to a theocratic revolution upon the delicate constitutional balance within the Saxon territories. More generally, by insisting on the princes' duty to protect the Gospel and the truly faithful, Müntzer was advocating and justifying a legal right of intervention which contravened the constitution of the Empire and the mandates of public peace.[50]

If the ernestine Saxon princes had any doubts about Müntzer's ultimate intentions, Luther was at hand to reassure them of their temporal authority. In his *Letter to the Princes of Saxony concerning the Rebellious Spirit* of mid-July Luther warned:

> Intending to resort to violence and the use of force against the authorities he will instigate revolt without delay.

In the face of rebellion the princes must exercise their divinely sanctioned office:

> Your obligation and duty to maintain order requires you to guard against such mischief and to prevent rebellion. Your Graces know very well that your power and earthly authority are given you by God in that you have been bidden to preserve the peace and to punish the wrongdoer, as Paul teaches, Romans 13.[51]

Luther likewise forestalled the charge that Müntzer might be guided by the Holy Spirit:

If, however, they attempt to justify themselves . . .
by saying that the Spirit impels them to achieve their
goal by resorting to force, I would reply: First, it must
be an evil spirit which has no other fruits than the
destruction of churches and cloisters and the burning
of images. . . . Secondly, their boasting about the
Spirit means nothing for we have the word of St John
that we should 'test the spirits to see whether they
are of God'. This spirit surely has not been tested,
but rages about and creates a furor with his
wantonness.[52]

The nub of the accusation levelled against Müntzer was
not that he preached false doctrine but that he espoused
violence:

As far as doctrine is concerned, time will tell. For the
present, your Graces ought not to stand in the way
of the ministry of the Word. Let them preach as
confidently and boldly as they are able and against
whomever they wish. For, as I have said, there must
be sects, and the Word of God must be under arms
and fight. . . . But when they want to do more than
fight with the Word, and begin to destroy and use
force, then your Graces must intervene . . . and
banish them from the country.[53]

Luther's denunciation was clouded by his own sense of
bitterness and rage that Müntzer should use the shelter
of electoral Saxony, the only territory then committed to
the Reformation, to attack the very man who had risked
his own life in first championing the reforming cause.

It speaks both for the princes' independence of mind
and for the impression which Müntzer may perhaps have
made on them in his *Sermon to the Princes* that, despite
Luther's alarm, they chose to proceed with caution and

with due regard for the law. On 31 July the Allstedt official, Hans Zeiß, Nickel Rucker, the magistrate, and two of the councillors were summoned along with Müntzer to an interrogation at Weimar. Over the next two days the councillors and Müntzer were questioned separately about recent events in Allstedt. For their part, Rucker and his colleagues tried, not surprisingly, to put the blame on Müntzer for causing the unrest. However understandable their stance, it ignored the inconvenient fact that Müntzer was not the only preacher in Allstedt: in the same cause Simon Haferitz had been just as outspoken. Yet not only was Haferitz not summoned to the hearing, he took advantage of Müntzer's absence to underscore their common purpose in a sermon which denounced all secular lords as knaves. Give them all they ask for, he declared, but then went on to urge his congregation to join the league and threatened future bloodshed.[54] When news of this sermon reached the authorities, a fresh interrogation of both preachers was immediately planned, but because of Müntzer's flight from Allstedt a week later it never took place. Whether Haferitz remained pastor of St Wigberti's after Müntzer's departure is unclear. According to Zeiß, Haferitz abjured Müntzer that August, and in subsequent years Luther was to give him his seal of approval as pastor in Magdeburg and Langensalza.[55] But in view of the overwhelming response which Müntzer's call for support evinced in Allstedt the following spring, it cannot be ruled out that Haferitz was still at his post, keeping Müntzer's torch aflame.

Of Müntzer's own testimony in Weimar only the bare bones survive. He denied preaching anything contrary to Scripture and exhorting the common people to form a league against the godless. Since he could hardly have abjured his solemn covenant so readily, there is good reason to think that he was in fact disclaiming any rebellious intentions thereby.[56] In accordance with his undertaking to the Saxon chancellor, Gregor Brück, on 13 July, Müntzer submitted for censorship the abbreviated version of his longest and most searching theological treatise, *A Manifest Exposé of False Faith*, which he was just completing.

The result of the interrogation was by no means a foregone conclusion. A chance encounter between Müntzer and Jakob Strauß, the reforming preacher of Eisenach and a determined opponent of usury and tithing, led to the latter proposing a colloquy of all the leading Saxon reformers – Luther, Melanchthon, Karlstadt, Müntzer, Strauß himself – to hammer out their differences. A public disputation, admittedly before an international forum, was, of course, what Müntzer had long demanded, and at first duke John was not altogether disinclined, not least because it would deprive Müntzer of any excuse to claim that he was banished on account of his doctrines.[57] In the meantime, on his return, Müntzer received an ultimatum from Zeiß at Allstedt castle on 3 August. He must close his printing-works, dismiss his printer, disband the Christian league, refrain from incendiary preaching and not obstruct the prosecution of the Mallerbach iconoclasts.

These orders were meant to muzzle Müntzer, and he knew it. Seething with rage he launched into a bitter tirade against the Saxon princes. Once he had calmed down he requested, and was granted, leave to address a final plea to the elector himself. In relatively measured tones and without resorting to threats, Müntzer conveyed his disapproval of 'fleshly and counterfeit benevolence' in a critical situation when 'Satan is driving the godless scholars to their downfall'. Luther's *Letter to the Princes of Saxony* he denounced as scandalous and mendacious. Beseeching Frederick to be allowed to continue preaching, he reaffirmed his willingness to submit his works to censorship, provided they were not judged by the 'poisonous and pompous biblical scholars alone'. Rather, he urged the elector to be guided by his own exposition of the Gospel of Luke (the shorter version of *A Manifest Exposé of False Faith*) and the letter of 22 July to Zeiß which explained 'the godly way to deal with any insurrection that may occur'.

Though Müntzer's appeal went unanswered the Saxon princes still refused to be rushed into precipitate action by Luther's call for banishment. But if they thought that Müntzer might knuckle under, they were mistaken: the conditions imposed upon him made a mockery of his ministry. Rather than submit, he chose to leave Allstedt of his own volition. On the night of 7 August he slipped over the town wall in the company of a goldsmith from Nordhausen, Martin Rüdiger, and headed southwestwards towards the imperial city of Mühlhausen in Thuringia, where the latter's family connections could offer him shelter. Müntzer's efforts to transform Allstedt into the new Jerusalem foundered upon the very rock which once had proved their greatest strength: an unshakeable conviction in the righteousness of his vision, both absolute and all-embracing, which brooked no religious compromise and acknowledged no political considerations.

Notes

1. Cf. Manfred Straube, 'Die politischen, ökonomischen und sozialen Verhältnisse des Amtes Allstedt in der ersten Hälfte des 16. Jahrhunderts' in Rat der Stadt Allstedt (ed.), *Allstedt – Wirkungsstätte Thomas Müntzers. Ein Beitrag zum 450. Jahrestag des deutschen Bauernkrieges 1975*, n.d., n.p.[Allstedt, 1975], 28–44.
2. A useful survey entitled 'Thomas Müntzer's liturgical experiments' is contained in R 305–23.
3. CW 176 f.

4. F 97 f (my translation).
5. Cf. Siegfried Bräuer and Wolfgang Ullmann (eds), *Thomas Müntzers Theologische Schriften aus dem Jahr 1523*, 2nd edn (Berlin, 1982), 52 ff.
6. In a letter to Georg [Amandus]. CW 104.
7. This phrase is contained only in the draft, not in the printed version. Ibid. 60.
8. Ibid. 61; cf. 63.
9. Cf. Michael G. Baylor, 'Thomas Müntzer's first publication', *Sixteenth Century Journal*, xvii (1986), 453.
10. CW 69.
11. Cf. Siegfried Bräuer, 'Die Vorgeschichte von Luthers "Ein Brief an die Fürsten zu Sachsen von dem aufrührerischen Geist" ', *Luther-Jahrbuch*, xlvii (1980), 49–50.
12. CW 196.
13. In Matheson's telling phrase. Ibid. 184.
14. Ibid. 219.
15. Ibid. 220.
16. Ibid. 223.
17. Ibid. 224.
18. Bräuer, 'Vorgeschichte', 54. The conference probably took place in the first week of March. Cf. Wieland Held, 'Der Allstedter Schosser Hans Zeiß und sein Verhältnis zu Thomas Müntzer', *Zeitschrift für Geschichtswissenschaft*, xxxv (1987), 1081.
19. From a letter of 13 May it appears that Müntzer may also have been present in Weimar. CW 75. It is certainly striking that the authorities referred to the events as 'Thomas Müntzer's affair'.
20. For the dating to 11 June, rather than 4 June (as E 429), cf. Bräuer, 'Vorgeschichte', 58 and Tom Scott, 'The "Volksreformation" of Thomas Müntzer in Allstedt and Mühlhausen', *Journal of Ecclesiastical History*, xxxiv (1983), 197, n. 12.
21. Reconstruction of events from documents in NM 159–65, 184. Cf. Scott, ' "Volksreformation" ', 197. The account in E 429–32 is very wayward.
22. CW 81.
23. Cf. NM 188–9.

24. CW 238 f.
25. Ibid. 244 f.
26. Ibid. 246.
27. Ibid. 248.
28. Ibid. 249.
29. Ibid. 93 f.
30. Ibid. 87.
31. Ibid. 88.
32. Ibid. 90.
33. Ibid. 96.
34. Ibid. 96.
35. It has been conclusively demonstrated by Bräuer that Hans Reichart was not, as had been supposed, Müntzer's printer in Allstedt. Siegfried Bräuer, 'Hans Reichart, der angebliche Allstedter Drucker Müntzers', *Zeitschrift für Kirchengeschichte*, LXXXV (1974), 389–98.
36. CW. 99.
37. The text in F 422 reads 'fronden' (*Fronen*: dues, renders), not 'fromden' (*Fremde*: strangers), but at ibid., n. 8, Franz acknowledges that *Fremde* must be meant on account of the reference to Matthew ch. 17 v. 26: do the kings of the earth take tribute from their own children, or from strangers? The original in Staatsarchiv Weimar, Reg. N 837, fo. 4r–5v should be read 'fromden'. The correct reading is important since it demonstrates clearly Müntzer's view that secular obedience was due even to godless rulers.
38. CW 102.
39. Siegfried Bräuer, 'Thomas Müntzer und der Allstedter Bund' in Jean-Georges Rott and Simon L. Verheus (eds), *Anabaptistes et dissidents au XVIᵉ siècle. Actes du Colloque international d'histoire anabaptiste du XVIᵉ siècle tenu à l'occasion de la XIᵉ Conférence Mennonite mondiale à Strasbourg, juillet 1984* (Bibliotheca Dissidentium, Scripta et Studia III) (Baden-Baden/Bouxwiller, 1987), 87–8. This dating now seems more plausible than my own suggestion that the 30-strong league represented the radical recasting at the end of April 1525 of the broad alliance of July 1524 as a revolutionary conspiracy, in response to Müntzer's urgent

appeal to his league members in Allstedt to rally to his side in the Peasants' War. Scott, ' "Volksreformation" ', 196.

40. AGBM II 756.
41. NM 181.
42. Ibid. 185.
43. On the Allstedt leagues cf. Bräuer, 'Allstedter Bund', 85–101, and Scott, ' "Volksreformation" ', 195 ff.
44. F 165 f. (my translation). Cf. Bräuer, 'Allstedter Bund', 94.
45. F 177–8 (my translation). Cf. Matthew ch. 26 v. 27–8.
46. Michael Müller, 'Die Gottlosen bei Thomas Müntzer – mit einem Vergleich zu Martin Luther', *Luther-Jahrbuch*, XLVI (1979), 97–119, esp. 107 ff.
47. W 48.
48. Cf. CW 434.
49. Bräuer, 'Allstedter Bund', 93.
50. W 49.
51. LW, vol. XL, 51.
52. Ibid. 52.
53. Ibid. 57.
54. NM 193.
55. Otto Clemen, 'Simon Haferitz' in idem, *Beiträge zur Reformationsgeschichte aus Büchern und Handschriften der Zwickauer Ratsschulbibliothek*, part II (Berlin, 1902), 23 ff. Müntzer's replacement was Jodocus Kern, a straightforward Lutheran.
56. E 496.
57. Ibid. 499.

4

From Allstedt to Mühlhausen

The flight from Allstedt plunged Müntzer into mental and emotional turmoil. Writing to the community which he had just forsaken Müntzer swithered between despondency and rage, resignation and recrimination. A short note to the council announcing his departure courteously reassured it that 'after a lengthy period of desolation, almighty God will come to you, imparting to you by his most loving will the fullness of illumination, provided that you do not deny him'. But hard on its heels came a philippic to the same address, full of bilious invective:

> Instead of the usual greeting I, Thomas Müntzer, wish the perverts among you a perverted God and the innocent among you a gracious and innocent fear of God.

All along, he declared, the councillors who had accompanied him to Weimar were plotting to abandon him to his fate:

> You know all too well you would have abandoned me to the cross. I will let the whole Christian people know one day how Nickel Rucker, that supreme

Judas Iscariot, and Hans Bosse and Hans Reichart
betrayed me, swearing by the saints to the prince that
they would have my neck, and not even blushing to
admit this before my very face at the castle. . . . Stir
it up, my dear lords, let the muck give out a good
old stink. I hope you will brew a fine beer out of it,
since you like drinking filth so much.[1]

It was just as well that this draft was never sent. In a
second draft[2] to the commons of Allstedt, however,
Müntzer stuck a calmer and more consoling note:

The enemies of the divine covenant . . . [take]
offence in the most materialistic way when true
progress takes place and the holy people of Christ
turns away with all its heart and soul from revering
the evil-doers in their fancy gear. . . . So pay no heed
if they take offence.

He appealed to them to renounce their fear of man and
accept the need for suffering:

But now that you are so afraid of the godless that
you, like the folk from Orlamünde, deny the
covenant of God, which you call the old and new
testament, there is nothing I can do. For you know
very well that subscribing [to the covenant] is not
directed against any government but only against
shameless tyranny. . . . Suffer for the sake of God. I
advise you to do this; otherwise you will have too
much to suffer for the sake of the devil.[3]

When Müntzer had at last roused himself sufficiently, he
despatched an apologia from Mühlhausen on 15 August
1524 intended for council and commons together,[4] which
was both conciliatory and defiant.

In my preaching to you I was moved to rebuke very sharply those tyrants over the Christian faith who, under the pretence of governing, put the people in chains and fetters to make them deny the Gospel. . . .

And now I have found it imperative to attack that other group which dared to defend such godless, abandoned men. . . . Yet all I really did was . . . to say that a Christian should not offer himself up so pitifully to the butcher's block, and that if the bigwigs do not stop this, one should take the reins of government away from them.

Müntzer comforted his flock and volunteered to remain at their service:

You wanted to elude the time of trial, but this is just impossible in an age like ours if we are to do what is right. Be of good courage: preaching like this cannot and will not take place without provoking an enormous scandal; for Christ himself is a stone of scandal. . . .

So on this occasion I will bid you farewell, since the circumstances demand this, in a friendly and gracious spirit, and I am most ready to be of service to you in all sincerity and with unfaltering diligence.[5]

In his hasty and clandestine departure – leaving behind his wife and child, his clerk and many of his papers, including his liturgies – Müntzer managed to stow amongst his few belongings the treatise upon which he had been working during the final weeks in Allstedt, *A Manifest Exposé of False Faith*. In a shorter and more temperate version – more probably abbreviation than preliminary draft[6] – it had already been submitted to the censors at the Weimar hearing under the title *The Testi-*

mony of the First Chapter of the Gospel of Luke. As a fugitive Müntzer was hard put to find a printer for the full text. He apparently entrusted the manuscript to Hans Hut from Bibra, a colporteur, who became his comrade-in-arms during the Peasants' War and thereafter a leader of the South German Anabaptists. Hut succeeded in delivering the work to Hans Hergot's radical printing-press in Nuremberg, where his apprentices brought out an edition of five hundred copies in their master's absence and without his permission. On its publication, however, the city's censor of religious tracts, Dominicus Schleupner, the Lutheran preacher of St Sebaldus parish church, ordered all the available copies to be confiscated; only those already sent to Augsburg, a batch of one hundred, ever went on sale.

The *Exposé* is the longest and most repetitious of Müntzer's tracts. At many stages it merely rehashes themes already developed in the *Prague Manifesto* and *On Counterfeit Faith*. The flow of argument is often uneven and unclear, a consequence, no doubt, of its dislocated composition. Theologically it offers little new. Nevertheless, the *Exposé* reveals subtle but significant shifts in Müntzer's thought as he drew the lessons of his ministry in Allstedt. For the first time his apocalyptic reading of history and his mystical theology were directly aligned, if not completely fused. For that purpose Luke's Gospel, with its eschatological overtones, was grist to his mill, not least the first chapter: he had already used the *Magnificat* in his *German Church Service*. Müntzer had begun to turn his attention from the princes to the common people, from the casting down of the mighty to the exaltation of the lowly. No longer did he pose as a new Daniel, the interpreter of the dreams of kings, but as a new John the Baptist, a voice crying in the wilderness to God's chosen people Israel.

The *Exposé* opens and closes with a demonstration of

the power of God's revelation. Neither Zechariah, the priest whose wife Elizabeth was too old and barren to bear a child, nor her cousin Mary, the virgin bride of Joseph, could at first believe the vision of the archangel Gabriel that Elizabeth would conceive a son and Mary become the mother of Christ. So the 'unbelief of all the elect was disclosed'.

> They did not arrive at their faith – as the foolish world does now – in a glossy, superficial way. They did not go about saying: 'Yes, all I need to do is believe, and God will bring it to pass.' The drunken world dreams up for itself a poisoned faith on such a frivolous basis, a faith that is much worse than that of the Turks, the pagans and the Jews. But Mary and Zechariah were seized by the fear of God until the mustard-seed of faith overcame their unbelief, of which they became aware in great fear and trembling.[7]

But that is not the faith taught by the inexperienced, untested biblical scholars who say 'quite unashamedly: "You see, I believe in Scripture!" They are worse than that idiot, the pope, with all his butter-boys',[8] in their prissy intellectualism which demands that ordinary folk seek their salvation in the written word.

> How cruelly this defrauds the poor and needy folk. For all their words and deeds ensure that the poor man is too worried about getting his food to have time to learn to read. Moreover they have the nerve to preach that the poor man should let himself be flayed and fleeced by the tyrants. . . . [9]

Müntzer was well aware of where such sentiments might lead, and he taunted his opponents with their likely response. 'Yes, yes, my dear Thomas, but you are getting too fanatical.' That only stirred him to spell out the full implication of his stance. If the biblical scholars served up a counterfeit faith to the common people, their daily grind in any case prevented them from recognising their unbelief. The misery of the common man was itself an injustice in the eyes of God:

> O God, the peasants are poor, care-worn folk. They have spent their life in a grim struggle for bread in order to fill the throats of the most godless tyrants. What chance have such poor, coarse folk of knowing anything.[10] . . . Usury and interest and dues prevent anyone coming to faith.[11]

'The spirit is only given to the poor in spirit (who recognise their unbelief),' and Müntzer was at last coming to identify and equate the poor in spirit with the downtrodden of this earth, the materially poor, the victims of the secular lords who 'fetter and shackle their people, flay and fleece them, menacing the whole people of Christ in the process, and cruelly torturing and killing their own subjects and others with ruthless severity'.

The present order, he declared, is not immutable. The godless can, and will, be torn from their judgement seats and the 'humble, coarse folk' raised in their stead. For the learned biblicists, however – Müntzer calls them *neutrales*, temporising hypocrites, and Luther in particular 'Brother Soft Life' and 'Father Pussyfoot' – that cannot happen until the Day of Judgement. 'They have the nerve to say that God never reveals his judgements. Hence they repudiate angels who are true messengers, coming . . . to divide the good from the evil.' The transformation of the world will come to pass when the poor common folk

learn to sigh, . . . to pray and long for a new John,

for a preacher full of grace, whose faith is solidly based on the experience of his unbelief.[12]

But they must on no account confound their longing for salvation with the fulfilment of creaturely desires. 'The common folk, too, will first have to be chided very severely about its unbridled lusts, which pass the time so intemperately and divertingly that there is no resolute will to take the faith earnestly.'

Müntzer's vision transcended the limited horizons of his unenlightened sympathisers: it was to restore the very order of creation. Just as Genesis described the act of creation, so Luke's Gospel testified to the new kingdom of Christ. 'Hence I say that if you are not prepared to learn the proper interpretation of the beginning of the Bible, then you will understand neither God nor the creatures nor the relationship between them.' But to those whose faith was truly born of the Holy Spirit through temptation, doubting and adversity, all things were possible.

> We must believe that we fleshly, earthly men are to become gods through Christ's becoming man and thus become God's pupils with him – to be taught by Christ himself, and become divine, yes, and far more – to be totally transfigured into him, so that this earthly life swings up into heaven.[13]

In that ringing declaration *A Manifest Exposé of False Faith* encapsulates everything that Müntzer in his Allstedt ministry had striven to achieve.

Haunted by the memory of his humiliating flight from Allstedt, Müntzer rounded upon the figure whose machinations, he believed, were ultimately responsible for what he now regarded as his expulsion. With no holds barred he savaged Luther in *A Highly Provoked Vindication and a*

Refutation of the Unspiritual Soft-Living Flesh in Wittenberg, 'whose robbery and distortion of Scripture has so grievously polluted our wretched Christian Church'. Conceived as a direct riposte to the *Letter to the Princes of Saxony concerning the Rebellious Spirit,* Müntzer's last tract may have been roughed out in Allstedt, but was not completed until late September after he had left Mühlhausen and arrived in Nuremberg. Even then he faced an uphill struggle to get it published. It was finally printed in late November or early December by another of the city's radical printers, Hieronymus Hölzel, but soon discovered by accident during a raid on the printing-works by officials searching for tracts by Karlstadt. This time the entire print-run was immediately impounded. Whether the handful of people who are ever likely to have read it could have made head or tail of its tortuous argument, which degenerates into a farrago of personal abuse, remains exceedingly doubtful. Yet amidst the incoherence and vituperation the *Vindication and Refutation* lays bare exactly why Müntzer had finally come to identify Wittenberg theology, not Catholic teaching, as the arch-pedlar of counterfeit faith.

Luther's dialectic of grace and faith – *sola gratia, sola fide* – was anathema to Müntzer. Faith is not a gift bestowed by grace alone, waiting to be plucked from God's hand by an act of sheer belief. Faith can only be achieved by wrestling with unbelief, through suffering, doubt and despair. The whole of Scripture cannot impart faith, as the learned biblicists insist:

If Christ is merely accepted on the testimony of the old and new covenants of God but preached without any manifestation of the spirit the result may be much more confusion and monkeying around than the Jews and the pagans caused.[14]

Scripture, rather, is the repository of the law, which Christ has come to fulfil. In showing man his unbelief, his disobedience to God's will, the law acts as an instrument of mortification: by killing our human will it manifests God's love for man, for it restores the true relationship between God and man, the state of grace contained within the original order of creation. By his easy reliance upon Scripture, Luther wilfully perverts its meaning:

> I refuse to tolerate his perverse way of treating the new covenant of God without first dealing with the divine commandments and the source of faith, which one can only reach after chastisement by the holy spirit, John 16. For it is only after the law is understood that the spirit punishes unbelief, which no one can understand until he has first embraced it himself, and as fiercely as the most unbelieving pagan. From the beginning, this is the way in which, testing themselves by the law, all the elect have come to understand their unbelief.[15]

But Müntzer goes further. The law is not merely corrective, it is also directive: God's will *shall* be done on earth as it is in heaven. It is the duty of the princes to execute God's will in the community by wielding the sword of justice. To ensure that the princes remain servants, not masters, of the sword, however, the community must control the sword:

> The power of the sword as well as the key to release sins is in the hands of the whole community. . . . The princes are not lords over the sword but servants of it. They should not act as they please, but execute justice, Deuteronomy 17. Hence it is a good old custom that the people must be present if someone is to be judged properly by the law of God, Numbers

15. Why? So that if the authorities try to give a corrupt judgement, Isaiah 10, the Christians present can object and prevent this happening, since anyone spilling innocent blood will be accountable to God, Psalm 78.[16]

Müntzer's disenchantment with temporal rulers for failing to discharge their sacred office is spelt out in the very next sentence. 'There is no greater abomination on earth than the fact that no one is prepared to take up the cause of the needy. The great do whatever they please.'

Their dereliction, Müntzer claimed, is grounded in material oppression.

Open your eyes! What is the evil brew from which all usury, theft and robbery springs but the assumption of our lords and princes that all creatures are their property? The fish in the water, the birds in the air, the plants on the face of the earth – it all has to belong to them. . . . To add insult to injury, they have God's commandment proclaimed to the poor. God has commanded that you should not steal. But it avails them nothing. For while they do violence to everyone, flay and fleece the poor farm worker, tradesman and everything that breathes, . . . should any of the latter commit the pettiest crime, he must hang. And Doctor Liar responds, Amen. It is the lords themselves who make the poor man their enemy. If they refuse to do away with the causes of insurrection how can trouble be avoided in the long run? If saying that makes me an inciter to insurrection, so be it![17]

Can Müntzer really have been surprised that his words were taken not as a warning but as a threat? And yet he was incensed that Luther should seize upon a letter to the Mansfeld miners written a few weeks earlier, which prophesied that they would shortly wash their hands in the blood of tyrants,[18] as proof of incitement to rebellion. Müntzer's reply, however, was scarcely calculated to dispel such fears.

All he [Luther] does is urge the mighty that no one should follow my teaching since it leads to insurrection. Anyone who wants to judge this matter fairly should neither love insurrection nor, on the other hand, should he be averse to a justified uprising. His outlook must be a balanced one.[19]

In other words, the elect must destroy the godless in righteous retaliation for their merciless oppression, in fulfilment of God's will, not their own.

Throughout his diatribe Müntzer displays an unrelenting obsession with Luther, 'that wily black crow', who becomes a veritable bogeyman. It is almost as if he was suffering from an inferiority complex towards an antagonist who he knew in the end would prevail. Touches of self-pity creep in: 'Without true or just cause he has made me a laughing-stock among his scornful, jeering, ruthless companions and has jeeringly reduced my name in the eyes of the simple, making me out to be a satan or a devil.' Only fleetingly does Müntzer emerge from his defensive corner to turn the tables on Luther.

Along came that Caiaphas, Doctor Liar, and gave his princes sound advice. He managed it splendidly, saying that he was worried about his fellow countrymen near Allstedt. As the whole land will testify on my account, the honest truth of the matter is this, that among the poor people there was such a thirst for truth that every road was crammed with people from far and near, who had come to hear how worship was conducted in Allstedt, with its Biblical praise and preaching. Although he nearly burst himself with his exertions he was unable to achieve anything of the sort in Wittenberg. One can see very well from his German Mass his holy rage about it. Indeed Luther was so vexed that he succeeded first of all in getting his prince to prohibit the printing of my liturgy.[20]

Thereafter the *Vindication and Refutation* peters out into rambling abuse and convoluted metaphors drawn from animal fables. It ends with a gruesome valediction:

Sleep softly, dear flesh! I would prefer to smell you roasting in your arrogance in a pot or in a cauldron by the fire . . . , smitten by God's wrath, and then stewing in your own juice. May the devil devour you! . . . Your flesh is like that of an ass; it would be a long time cooking and would turn out to be a tough dish indeed for your mealy-mouthed friends.[21]

Müntzer had burnt his boats. With the *Vindication and Refutation* he severed all remaining links with the official Reformation in Saxony and with its sponsors, the ernestine princes. Religiously and politically he had reached the point of no return, a martyr to his own transcendent vision. His last letters to the people of Allstedt were signed 'Thomas Müntzer, a servant of God'. It was that sense of mission which sustained him in adversity as he crossed the borders of Saxony to find shelter in Mühlhausen. The contrast between the quiet little Saxon town, upon which he had left so deep a mark, and the much larger city, already in the throes of political and religious upheaval, could scarcely have been greater.

As an imperial city Mühlhausen owed allegiance to the Emperor alone, although its political independence was compromised by the proximity of large princely territories – those of the archbishops of Mainz, the electors of Saxony, and the Saxon dukes. In the previous century it had been obliged to sign unwelcome protective agreements with both the Saxon duchies and with the landgraviate of Hessen. By the beginning of the sixteenth century Mühlhausen was the second largest city of Thuringia after Erfurt, with up to 8500 inhabitants. Another 2500 or so subjects lived in seventeen villages scattered round the city in a small rural territory which formed a modest counterweight to Mühlhausen's powerful neighbours. Despite its size, its prosperity was declining in the face of competition from new commercial centres to the east, notably Leipzig, which left Mühlhausen and Thuringia in the west increasingly cut off from the major arteries of trade. As a consequence, the fragile political balance in a commune characterised by considerable social division and dominated by an oligarchy drawn from the minority of enfranchised burghers was upset, as the commons pressed their economic grievances upon the council.

From 1523 onwards Mühlhausen was seized by internal strife as the middling craftsmen in the guilds vied with the council for proper political representation. The commons' opposition was spurred on by the city's leading agitator and reforming preacher, Heinrich Schwertfeger, called Pfeiffer, a native of the city and former monk, who had already attracted a considerable following amongst the lesser populace by anticlerical invective delivered from the pulpit of his parish church St Nicholas in the southwestern suburbs. The council's attempts to have Pfeiffer expelled backfired, for on 1 April 1523 a new citizens' assembly of forty men was set up, which appointed an eight-strong delegate committee to oversee public business. After rioting at the beginning of July the council was forced to adopt the Mühlhausen Recess, in effect a new constitution which guaranteed the committee of Eight a permanent voice in civic affairs, ordained that the town's parishes be staffed by evangelical preachers, and abolished the clergy's fiscal immunities.[22]

In spite of its far-reaching provisions the Recess failed to restore calm to the city; on the contrary, it gave Pfeiffer and his associates room to press their reforming demands further and to whip up popular feeling against the convents and clergy. In August Pfeiffer was in fact banished temporarily for inciting public disorder, but when he returned in December he resumed his anticlerical attacks, and in the early months of 1524 fresh iconoclastic outbursts occurred against the church of the Dominicans. Mühlhausen, therefore, seemed to offer fertile ground for Müntzer to relaunch his religious crusade.

He immediately applied for a licence to preach, but the council was uncertain of his credentials. Despite its reservations permission was quickly granted – presumably because the terms of the Recess left the city fathers no alternative – though subsequent warnings from Luther and the Saxon authorities caused them to regret their decision. By mid-August Müntzer was writing to Allstedt, to have his 'mass- and vesper-books' sent on and summoning his clerk to join him. Müntzer's wife and child, it appears, followed shortly thereafter with the family belongings. By his own account, Müntzer found the populace rather backward in faith, though at least they had not, in his eyes, been corrupted by Lutheran influences.

The people in Mühlhausen are slow, for here as elsewhere the folk are rather uncouth; this is God's deliberate design, lest their mother wit should block the way of the Gospel. It may help my cause in places like this, for where cleverness abounds, deviousness abounds too.[23]

Nothing is known about his contacts with Pfeiffer in the first few weeks, though the latter seems to have accepted the arrival of a more prominent and outspoken reformer without demur. By early September, at any rate, they had made common cause. Thenceforth they worked hand-in-glove to bring about the radical transformation of Mühlhausen into a true city of God. After further attacks upon religious foundations in mid-September, in which altarpieces were smashed and reliquaries destroyed, seemingly with Müntzer's blessing,[24] an incident on Monday 19 September at last provided the two preachers with the pretext they needed to unleash a full-scale campaign of political agitation designed to unseat the existing council and usher in a new godly regime.

At a wedding that day one of the city's two mayors, Sebastian Rodemann, had a court-clerk arrested for drunkenness and thrown into gaol at the town hall, in flagrant contravention of the Recess's provisions against arbitrary imprisonment. The committee of Eight managed to secure his release, and tried to call Rodemann, together with his colleague Johann Wettich, to book. Though both mayors swore to answer charges the next day, when the time came they slipped out of town and headed south to Langensalza, taking with them the city's flag, seals, keys, and a horse.[25] The previous evening Müntzer and Pfeiffer, carrying a red cross and holding aloft a naked sword, led more than two hundred of their followers on a march out of the city as far as a wayside chapel at Eiche, where they pitched camp for the night, returning to Mühlhausen the following morning.[26] On the Tuesday further disturbances ensued, partly in front of the town hall, which led to ten other councillors fleeing the city, and partly around the Felchta gate in Pfeiffer's parish of St Nicholas. Renewed bouts of rioting erupted over the next three days. The upshot was that Müntzer's and Pfeiffer's faction, probably on Tuesday, drew up heads of demands – the so-called Eleven Articles – which they circulated within the city and its dependent villages. These articles called for the installation of a new council which should act solely according to God's law as revealed in Scripture, so that arbitrary and oppressive rule might yield to government in accordance with the commonweal.

On Wednesday 21 September the remaining councillors and members of the Eight sent without success to Langensalza to recover the city's insignia, whilst the commons foregathered in their separate wards to discuss the next moves, though they failed to agree on a common course of action. In this volatile situation Müntzer issued the next day a public declaration to the 'Church' in Mühlhausen, setting forth the reasons why the council should be dismissed from office.

> It is now quite clear to me that the fear of men is what prevents you from coming to any decisions. Now that almighty God has written up for you in clear, bold lettering the faults, crimes, outrages of your authorities and the whole variety of ways in which they are leading you astray, it is only right that you should make them face up to this, . . . admonishing them fraternally that to avoid the evil to come they should, for God's sake, accept their dismissal in the interests of you all.[27]

He made no mention of violent action if the councillors should prove stubborn. Instead he proposed that the commons do their duty towards God by publicising their accusations to all the world, so that they be recognised as God's long-suffering elect.

So if it does appear in print for the whole world to see, then you can count on the understanding of all Christian people. They will say: Look, these pious folk have shown far too much patience. They have kept to the divine commandment. So the Christian people will speak of you as an elect people, Deuteronomy 4, 'Look, this is a wise people, it is a discerning people; a great people will arise from it. It is a people that will hazard all for God. It will do what is right and will not fear the devil or the world with all its plots, devices and pomposity'.[28]

Should they ignore his advice, he warned, 'You will have to suffer for the sake of the devil what, with God on your side, you could have endured easily.'

Müntzer's appeal brought no immediate response, though unrest in the city continued unabated. Over the weekend, however, two astonishing incidents occurred. On Saturday 24 September peasants from Mühlhausen's dependent villages assembled to rebuke the commons for their allegedly unchristian behaviour, and threatened to seek a new overlord unless matters improved. The following evening the peasants of Bollstedt, south-east of Mühlhausen, received warning that their village was about to be set on fire, and on the Monday morning it duly went up in flames with the loss of a large stock of corn. The council was on the verge of sending help when it received a message which caused it to shut the gates and summon the populace to the town hall. There was evidently uproar in the city for, as the ducal Saxon official in Langensalza, Sittich von Berlepsch, reported, a preacher had arrived on Luther's instructions to denounce Müntzer, and each side was calling the other heretics and knaves.[29] At that point the parishioners of St Nicholas raised a crucifix which they paraded round the city, declaring that whoever stood by the passion and Gospel of Christ should gather in the suburb. Thereupon they seized the Felchta gate and kept it open, whilst all the others remained barred.

Whilst representatives from the neighbouring imperial cities of Goslar and Nordhausen and the former imperial city of Erfurt tried to mediate in the crisis, the council sought to strengthen its shaky hold upon affairs by calling up reinforcements from its villages. Of the two hundred peasants who were marshalled, some, however, went over to the commons' opposition so that the council found itself sending all but sixty home again. It also appointed two new mayors to replace Rodemann and Wettich. In the meantime Pfeiffer, to forestall expulsion, had led a party of his followers out of the city, whereupon the council closed the Felchta gate behind them and posted a picket to guard it for the rest of the day, though in the evening the rebels tried to storm it until beaten back by artillery. The next morning, Tuesday 27 September, the council decided – or was forced – to reopen the Felchta gate, which enabled Pfeiffer and his supporters to gain readmittance. The council then summoned the entire citizenry to muster at the town hall, and took oaths of renewed fealty in the square by the Franciscan church from many of the dissidents, including men from the suburb of St Nicholas. Having formally reasserted its authority, the council tried to establish a consensus by canvassing opinion in the city wards. A majority voted to eject Müntzer and Pfeiffer, who had no choice but to depart. As the two preachers took their leave they were escorted by many followers. The week-long crisis in Mühlhausen was over.

Müntzer's part in these events appears curiously muted. The sources almost invariably refer to agitation by Pfeiffer and his suburban following, though at the outset Sittich von Berlepsch sardonically referred to 'the foolish priest from Allstedt' who was instructing the populace to withdraw allegiance from all authority, to withhold rents and interest-payments, and to expel the Catholic clergy. In all likelihood this gives a somewhat garbled account of Müntzer's plans, despite the echoes of earlier agitation against Naundorf and the programme of the smaller Allstedt league. Müntzer steps into the limelight only with the march to Eiche and his letter to the 'Church' of Mühlhausen, though he certainly had a hand in drafting the Eleven Articles as well. The purpose of the march to Eiche on 19 September remains a mystery; it so uncannily resembles the sequence of events the following Monday when Pfeiffer fled the city that there must be some suspicion that accounts of the latter and perfectly explicable action have become unravelled into two separate incidents on successive Mondays. Yet the evidence for two events is incontrovertible: there is no room for confusion over the dating.[30] The march to Eiche can only be interpreted as a symbol of religious defiance, similar to the parade of the crucifix through the city a week later, but whether the wayside shrine was desecrated by the marchers, echoing the Mallerbach affair, remains alas unknown. The march has a much wider significance, however, inasmuch as it is commonly held to mark the formation of a new Christian league by Müntzer, bent upon reviving in Mühlhausen what he had had to abandon in Allstedt.

It is quite true that Müntzer founded the so-called 'Eternal League of God' in Mühlhausen, whose origins appear at first sight to coincide with the crisis of mid-September 1524. An undated list of members of this league records 219 names, a figure which tallies closely with the number of those who are known to have joined the march to Eiche.[31] Moreover, the list was drawn up outside the Felchta gate, the headquarters of Müntzer's and Pfeiffer's opposition.[32] There are strong grounds for thinking, however, that the Eternal League was not in fact established until much later.[33] By mid-September 1524

Müntzer had been in Mühlhausen barely a month and
had yet to find a permanent post from which to proclaim
his message, so that his chances of harnessing the long-
standing communal opposition to his cause were necessarily restricted. In any case, there is no reference to the
Eternal League in the sources until April 1525, when its
organisation was described by Sittich von Berlepsch who
had himself previously reported the march to Eiche in
some detail without mentioning a league. That alone
would seem to preclude its foundation in the autumn of
1524. But the most telling piece of evidence against a
September dating is provided by Müntzer's own letter to
the Church in Mühlhausen three days after the march, in
which he makes no allusion to a league, eternal or otherwise, despite the obvious opportunity to urge support
amongst the citizens at large. The Eternal League ought
more properly to be assigned, therefore, to the agitation
stirred up by Müntzer against the newly appointed
Eternal Council the following spring.[34]

The letter to the Church in Mühlhausen exists only in
copy, appended to a submission by the linenweavers on
how the city should be governed. Müntzer clearly
intended it as a general exhortation to accompany the
specific demands contained in the Eleven Articles, which
in several places echo its language, notably in the threat
that the council's transgressions should be exposed in
print. Some confusion surrounds the precise relationship
between all three documents, however, not least because
only Müntzer's letter carries a date. The Eleven Articles,
which survive in the version sent to Mühlhausen's village
of Horsmar, were addressed to the entire populace of city
and territory on behalf of three suburban parishes, St
Nicholas (Pfeiffer's own), St George and St Margaret,
together with the linenweavers of St Jacob just inside the
Felchta gate. There can be no doubt that they constitute a
revolutionary programme which would have transformed

Mühlhausen into a purified Christian community of the elect. The first two articles are vintage Müntzer, brimming with biblical references:

[1.] That a completely new council be appointed. Why? To ensure that actions are taken in the fear of God; that old hatreds do not linger on; that arbitrariness ceases; since the evil doer and the dispenser of justice deserve equal punishment; Romans 1, Luke 19 on the self-willed servant; lest there be a half-baked mixture of those outside and those inside; from which the community is bound to suffer, for it is a hard thing to have judges who are themselves guilty.
[2.] That righteousness and judgement be exercised in accordance with the Bible or command of the holy word of God. Why? To ensure that the poor are treated in the same way as the rich, as in Zechariah 17, Leviticus 19 and 26, John 7, Matthew 5, Luke 18.[35]

The Articles then elaborate how the councillors are to govern. They shall not be appointed for a fixed term, and no one shall be compelled to serve. They shall be adequately remunerated; they shall use the new city seal. With God's word as its guiding principle the council shall at all times serve the commonweal. Given his long-standing involvement in Mühlhausen's communal opposition, Pfeiffer may well be responsible for the practical details of installing the new council, with Müntzer in a subordinate role supplying some of the phraseology and scriptural citation. It is certainly worth noting that the Eleven Articles envisage magistrates, rather than a clerical board, and they offer no role, advisory or mandatory, to a prophetic leader, be he a new Elijah, Daniel, or John the Baptist. There is nothing in the Articles to foreshadow

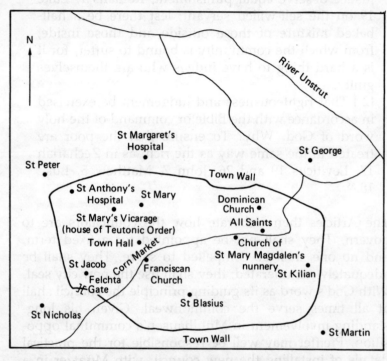

MAP 5 The Imperial Free City of Mühlhausen

Calvin's Geneva, let alone the Anabaptist kingdom of Zion in Münster. They remain at best an uneasy amalgam of late medieval secular traditions of urban popular protest and radical evangelical theology.

The radical tone of the Eleven Articles is sustained in the separate submission of the linenweavers, who demanded that a new council be appointed and sworn in which would govern according to 'God's command, and the holy books of holy Scripture'. All existing constitutional provisions, whether in terms of the Recess or imperial law, should only be valid, they insisted, in so far as they conformed to Scripture.[36] For that reason the submission – which itself only survives as an incomplete copy – has been seen as a deliberate attempt by a section of Müntzer's and Pfeiffer's following to put pressure on the council to bend to the popular will. That presupposes, however, that it was drafted at the same time as Müntzer's letter to the Christians of Mühlhausen at the height of the crisis, whereas both form and content suggest that it was one of the responses taken by the revamped council on 27 September, as the work of pacification got under way.[37] That may well explain the rather plaintive codicil which requests the right to compose and submit articles of grievance to Mühlhausen's appointed advisors within the Empire and other recognised cities.[38] Such sentiments seem very far removed from Müntzer's invocation of the fear of God.

Considering the history of popular unrest in Mühlhausen and Pfeiffer's undoubted following, the failure of the communal movement in September 1524 is all the more striking. The truth is that the commons' opposition was split. The moderate faction of middling burghers, originally led by Pfeiffer, which had been victorious in 1523, merely demanded a share in political power through the committee of Eight, and the reform of clerical abuses. By late 1524, however, Pfeiffer's growing radicalism, stimulated no doubt by Müntzer's presence, had estranged some of his earlier support whilst entrenching the loyalty of the mass of poorer inhabitants, especially in the suburbs and plebeian districts, who were just as scathing about the Eight as about the old council.[39] That emerges quite plainly from the course of events. The street demonstrations on 20 September were clearly the work of two separate factions, the moderates at the town hall and the radicals under the two preachers, who made the Felchta gate the centre of their resistance throughout the entire week. The latter certainly succeeded in panicking the council to the point of troops being called up from the villages, and they kept the agitation going even after it transpired that their following was far from universal.

The most remarkable feature of the September unrest, however, was the reluctance of Mühlhausen's seventeen villages to rally to the communal opposition in substantial numbers. Their public protest on 24 September against the commons' 'unchristian behaviour' and their readiness to come to the beleaguered council's aid stand in startling contrast to the strands of opposition within Mühlhausen itself. It cannot be because they were hostile towards the new religious doctrines. On the contrary, Mühlhausen's two richest villages, Görmar and Ammern, had earlier that spring driven out their Catholic priests in favour of evangelical preachers. From 1523 onwards Pfeiffer had been building up a following, moreover, in the Eichsfeld north-west of the city, and it is at least conceivable that the aim of the radicals' march to the chapel at Eiche on the first Monday of the crisis may have been to enlist some or all of Mühlhausen's villages in a common struggle against the civic authorities. The Eleven Articles were distributed for that very purpose. The explanation lies in the Articles themselves, which contain only the demands of the popular movement in the city itself and ignore any rural grievances that the villagers might have harboured. The eleventh and final article, indeed, is in reality not a demand at all but a peremptory injunction to the peasants couched in language both patronising and offensive:

[11.] In this whole matter we want action taken without vacillation, without any delay, and in accordance with the word of God. Why? If the execution of God's commands is to be thwarted, then we want you to tell us what our dear Lord and his only Son Jesus Christ, together with the Holy Spirit, has done to you, to make you unwilling to have him overrule your wretched sack of worms? In what way has he lied to you, or betrayed you? For he is righteous. . . .[40]

Seen in this light the villagers' angry assembly on Saturday 24 September emerges as the understandable reaction to the despatch of the Eleven Articles, which must therefore have been drawn up towards the end of that week. By the same token, the burning of Bollstedt at dawn the following Monday looks like a particularly vicious reprisal for the villagers' stubborn refusal to join forces. Though there is no conclusive evidence to link it to the radical plebeian opposition, rumour had it that 'those who had carried the letter [that is, the Eleven Articles] out of the city' were indeed responsible for setting fire to several barns in the village.[41]

Müntzer's first sojourn in Mühlhausen had ended in a threefold failure. He had failed to set his unique religious stamp upon the communal opposition; its agitation had failed to overthrow the existing council despite its precarious control; and the lowly followers of himself and Pfeiffer had failed to forge a common bond with Mühlhausen's dependent peasantry despite intimidation. After the success of his ministry in Allstedt the month in

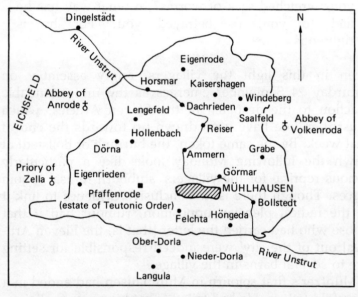

MAP 6 Mühlhausen and its Territory

Mühlhausen must have been a bitter disappointment. Though Pfeiffer managed to return to his native city in December, Müntzer was unable to gain readmittance until the following spring. His family seems to have remained in Mühlhausen whilst Müntzer was cast adrift with winter fast approaching. His renewed experience of poverty and desolation served only to convince him that his apocalyptic expectation of the transformation of the world would shortly be fulfilled.

Notes

1. CW 114.
2. The language and contents of the two drafts make plain that they were addressed to different recipients.
3. Ibid. 115.
4. Ibid. 116.
5. Ibid. 117.
6. Cf. ibid. 254 f.
7. Ibid. 266–8.
8. I.e. those who had been granted indulgences to eat butter during Lent.
9. Ibid. 272.
10. Ibid. 294.
11. Ibid. 304.
12. Ibid. 296.
13. Ibid. 278.
14. Ibid. 330.
15. Ibid. 332 f.
16. Ibid. 334 f.
17. Ibid. 335.
18. NM 203.
19. CW 341.
20. Ibid. 338 f.
21. Ibid. 348.
22. AGBM II 10–15.
23. CW 120 f.

24. G I 748–9.
25. J 179–80.
26. G I 749–50.
27. CW 132 f.
28. Ibid. 133.
29. G I 749.
30. Compare J 180–1 with G I 749–50.
31. Staatsarchiv Dresden, Loc. 9135. Acta den Aufruhr zu Mühlhausen betreffend, I, fo. 44 r–v; 47 r–v.
32. Kreisarchiv Mühlhausen, 1–10/K 3 13, fo. 121v. Confession of Claus Tuchscherer (or Haldecke), 11 May 1526. This passage is omitted in AGBM II 827–8.
33. Cf. E 577, n. 39; Scott, ' "Volksreformation" ', 202.
34. The surviving list of members is not a reliable guide since it is obviously a fair copy, which makes it impossible to tell when it was drawn up. At all events, it cannot date from the original recruitment outside the Felchta gate, since it concludes with the names of three members described as expelled. These names cannot, in turn, have been added later, since the list is written all-of-a-piece by one hand without evident pause or variation of pen or ink. Moreover, the richest member listed, Hans Linse, who was one of the new mayors appointed to replace Rodemann and Wettich, is unlikely to have been a founder member of any September league, since the following week he was apparently content to preside over Müntzer's and Pfeiffer's expulsion! The most recent East German analysis of the Eternal League regrettably ignores these points. Cf. Eckhart Leisering, 'Die Anhänger Thomas Müntzers in Mühlhausen' (Diplomarbeit Geschichtswissenschaft, University of Leipzig, 1986).
35. CW 455 f.
36. AGBM II 49.
37. Scott, ' "Volksreformation" ', 203, n. 49.
38. AGBM II 50.
39. Cf. Article 6 of the Eleven Articles. CW 456 f.
40. Ibid. 458. The German original speaks of maggots, not worms!
41. Kreisarchiv Mühlhausen, 1–10/K 3 3 und 9, fo. 82v.

Confession of Jacob Hoppe, [2 October] 1528. The relevant passage is omitted in AGBM II 911–12.

5
The Peasants' War

After his expulsion Müntzer's itinerary is not easy to unravel. Pfeiffer, it appears, headed straight for Nuremberg, where he soon attracted the attention of the city council by engaging in public debate on matters of religion. With him he carried two pamphlets, one an account of the September uprising in Mühlhausen, the other an exposition of biblical law and its judgement on false prophets, which clearly chimes with the concerns expressed by Müntzer in the *Vindication and Refutation*. These tracts were enough to have Pfeiffer banished at the end of October, when he returned to Thuringia to campaign in the countryside around Mühlhausen for readmittance to the city. Whether Müntzer accompanied Pfeiffer directly to the Franconian capital remains uncertain, but there is little doubt that he spent some time in the city in October or November.[1] On his own testimony he received invitations to preach, which he declined on the grounds that his purpose in the city was to get his works published. This is by no means implausible, since he may well have needed time to finish the *Vindication and Refutation*. What is remarkable, however, is that Müntzer – unlike Pfeiffer – was able to escape detection for several weeks in a city notorious for surveillance of its own citizenry through an elaborate system of spies and informers. The only immediate explanation – that he was protected by friends in high places – is borne out by recent research which has uncovered correspondence between Müntzer and Christoph Fürer, a scion of one of Nuremberg's leading patrician families and a member of the city council. His links with Fürer can be traced back to the extensive network of contacts amongst international merchants, particularly those involved in the mining industry, which Müntzer had established during his early years in Brunswick. Fürer was himself a mining entrepreneur with business contacts in Thuringia, where for a time he had acted as the agent for various smelting and refining companies. It seems highly probable, therefore, that Müntzer found shelter with Fürer during his stay in Nuremberg which enabled him to complete his writing undisturbed.[2]

Though Müntzer remained in deliberate seclusion in Nuremberg, he may have made contact with the rector of the St Sebaldus school, Hans Denck, a theologian who was to become, alongside Hans Hut, the leader of the South German spiritualist Anabaptists. Denck was certainly influenced by Müntzer's mystical theology, but recoiled from his bloodthirsty advocacy of a final reckoning with the godless on this earth. After his expulsion from Nuremberg in January 1525 on account of his radical religious views, Denck found a teaching post in Mühlhausen, though whether either Müntzer or Pfeiffer had a hand in the appointment is impossible to tell. If the two men did meet, it may have been Denck who encouraged Müntzer to travel much further southwards to Basel on the Upper Rhine where his old tutor, Johannes Oecolampadius, was professor of theology at the university.

On the assumption that Müntzer left Nuremberg around the third week of November, he would have arrived in Basel at the beginning of December, where he had two meetings with Oecolampadius. On the first occasion Müntzer did not give his name, pleading that he was a refugee, but when Oecolampadius invited him for a meal he turned up in the company of a young and enthusiastic Swiss humanist, Ulrich Hugwald, and a long theological discussion then ensued, during which Müntzer at last revealed his identity. Our knowledge of these encounters rests upon Oecolampadius's own account contained in a couple of letters written well after the events they were describing. At the best of times a timid man, Oecolampadius was naturally concerned to play down the significance of the meetings and any strong impression which Müntzer might have left upon him. Much of the conversation revolved around Müntzer's distinctive theology of the Cross with its emphasis on the receipt of the Holy Spirit through suffering, and they discussed a recent tract of his, probably *A Manifest Exposé of False Faith*. Finally they turned to the Sacraments, in which Müntzer apparently said little about either baptism or the Mass which struck his host as radically at variance with orthodox reforming sentiments.[3]

According to his later confession, Müntzer was encouraged by Oecolampadius and Hugwald to journey further up the Rhine towards Lake Constance, where the first rumblings of widespread peasant disaffection had occurred that summer. The two Swiss scholars doubtless saw it as a unique opportunity for Müntzer to preach his visionary message in a region in the grip of Zwinglian reforming doctrines emanating from Zürich, and influenced by the Anabaptist ministry of Balthasar Hubmaier in the little Austrian town of Waldshut on the Rhine. In all, Müntzer may have spent up to eight weeks in the Klettgau and Hegau, the Austrian territories immediately to the west of Lake Constance; during that time he travelled the surrounding countryside from his base in the village of Grießen in the heart of the Klettgau. There is no direct evidence that he had contact with Hubmaier in

Waldshut, though the subsequent course of events makes it highly probable. Whether he also received a delegation of those Zürich radicals, led by Conrad Grebel, whose long letter on theological issues addressed to him in Allstedt at the beginning of September had been returned undelivered (if indeed it was ever sent), remains entirely unknown.

All in all, the details of Müntzer's fugitive and vagabond existence in South-West Germany are extraordinarily sparse. It is surely astonishing that his name crops up nowhere in the surviving sources, neither in Hubmaier's or Zwingli's correspondence, nor in the despatches of the feudal authorities or the peasants' own submissions. The only letter of Müntzer's to survive between September 1524 and March 1525 is a report to his friend, Christoph Meinhard, in Eisleben, the cousin of the Allstedt official, Hans Zeiß, on his treatment in Nuremberg, which pleads desperate poverty: 'If you can manage it, help me with my sustenance in any way you can.' And yet Müntzer remained in contact with the South-West German peasants after his return to Saxony: by his own account, he had kept their letters to him in a sack which his wife, Ottilie von Gersen, was looking after in Mühlhausen.

In his enforced confession, however, Müntzer admitted that during his stay in the Klettgau and Hegau he had composed 'some articles, drawn from the Gospel, on how one should govern, from which, later on, other articles were devised'.[4] What were these articles? Do they contain a programme, not merely a framework, of godly rule on earth? Had Müntzer at last taken the fateful step from visionary theologian to social revolutionary? The articles do not survive in the original, but they may be reconstructed from documents found in Hubmaier's possession after his flight from Waldshut in November 1525. That does not, of course, prove that Müntzer and Hubmaier

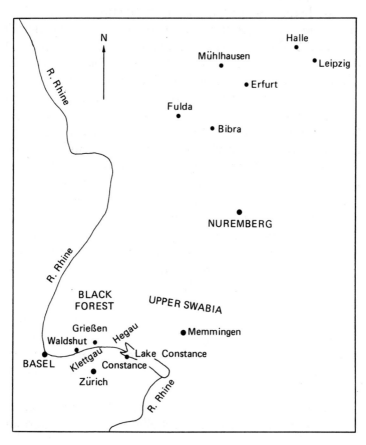

MAP 7   Müntzer's Journey to South-West Germany

met – how widely the articles were circulated is unknown – but it makes it more likely. Unfortunately, the bundle of Hubmaier's papers does not itself survive. Its contents are paraphrased in a report sent to duke George of Saxony in March 1528 by Johann Fabri, the bishop of Constance's erstwhile vicar-general. Because it was intended to discredit Hubmaier, who had just been burnt by the Catholic hierarchy in Vienna as a heretic, Fabri's account has commonly been presumed tendentious. Certainly Fabri, by then bishop of Vienna, could not be expected to give a dispassionate account of Hubmaier's doctrines, but he was present in Waldshut after its capitulation in late 1525 and had direct knowledge of the peasants' uprising.[5] Amongst Hubmaier's papers, according to Fabri, were two documents which have always been regarded as central to the Peasants' War in South-West Germany – the *Constitutional Draft* and the *Letter of Articles*.

Historians have long puzzled over the correct interpretation of the two documents and their relationship to each other. At various times both Müntzer and Hubmaier have been advanced as the author of either one or the other. Recent research has gone far towards unravelling the complex questions of composition and intention, but its findings cannot easily be recounted without the risk of distortion. It is necessary, therefore, to trace the history of the *Constitutional Draft* and the *Letter of Articles* step-by-step. Only then will Müntzer's activity in South-West Germany and the lessons which he drew for his subsequent involvement in rebellion in central Germany become fully apparent.

Fabri himself declined to spell out the provisions of the *Letter of Articles* since they contained 'so many unchristian clauses and seditiousness', but he gave a précis of the secular ban which was attached to it. There is no difficulty in identifying the document, however, since Fabri's description matches a copy of the *Letter of Articles* – with an explanation of the secular ban appended – in the possession of the Black Forest peasant army in the spring of 1525.[6] The *Constitutional Draft*, on the other hand, poses much more of a problem. Fabri gives a text which, as it stands, is neither complete nor original, but no other version has ever been found with which to compare it. Even the title is a later and somewhat misleading historian's invention. And yet in the *Constitutional Draft* may be discerned, despite omissions and reworkings, the core of Müntzer's articles on how to govern. The *Draft* contains four clauses in Fabri's rendering:

[1.] And teaches therein that the people of each region (*Landschaft*) shall come together and make a league. The time has already come when God will no longer suffer the secular lords' flaying, fleecing, fettering, shackling, grinding, binding and other tyranny. They deal with the poor folk as Herod with the innocent children. As the murderous duke of Lorraine has given us a first taste of His Princely Grace at Saverne and elsewhere. So that this be stopped, the people must come together to make an ordinance according to God's word.

[2.] Therefore the commons (*Gemein*) shall write to its lords once, twice and thrice that they shall join its brotherhood and union. If they will not join, then each region shall be allowed to take the sword from its lords and give it to another. If the region does not do so, it is conniving in the lords' depravity.

[3.] And teaches how to appoint kings, princes, dukes and territorial lords. Namely, when the people is foregathered, it shall vow together to keep God's word, and from twelve men put forward by the peasants shall chose one, with no special regard to be given to the nobility. And should the man chosen

thereafter prove unsuitable, he may be deposed after
the region has cautioned him thrice. For this the
region shall pledge its members to stake and shed
their body, honour, goods and blood all together.

[4.] But should the deposed lords seek revenge, he
teaches in the fourth chapter, the new lord shall place
them under the secular ban, and if the ban has no
effect, the new territorial lord shall levy his land or
hire mercenaries at the region's expense and fall
upon the obstinate, till the bloodthirsty tyrants be
extirpated.[7]

The echoes of Müntzer's language and style are impossible to miss. The 'flaying, fleecing, fettering and shackling'
of the common people, the analogy with Herod come
straight from *A Manifest Exposé of False Faith*.[8] The doctrine
of the sword and the threat to extirpate the tyrants are
also undiluted Müntzer. Nevertheless, there are several
obstacles in the way of any direct attribution to Müntzer.
The secular ban described in the fourth clause is not part
of Müntzer's thought, though it features prominently in
the *Letter of Articles*. Its source must surely lie with
Hubmaier, whose doctrine of the spiritual or Christian
ban runs throughout his writings.[9] Though Hubmaier
never uses the term 'secular ban' there can be little doubt
that it represents a conscious application of the spiritual
ban to the problem of a recalcitrant overlord who resists
the word of God.[10] Another discrepant feature is the
concept of the region (*Landschaft*), which is alien to
Müntzer's writings and has specifically South German or
Swiss connotations as the commons of a territory or its
political assembly.[11] More puzzling still is the reference to
duke Anthony of Lorraine's slaughter of the Alsatian
rebels at Saverne on 16 May 1525, long after Müntzer
had left South-West Germany, indeed the very day after

Müntzer had led the Saxon and Thuringian peasant armies to defeat at the battle of Frankenhausen. The allusion strikes an entirely discordant note in the first clause, however, and is beyond doubt a later, and despairing, gloss.[12]

At the very least, therefore, the *Constitutional Draft* cannot be regarded as the original version of Müntzer's articles, though it is tempting to relate the obvious additions and reworkings to the 'other articles' which, as he acknowledged, had subsequently been derived from them. A close reading of Fabri's own description of the Hubmaier packet reveals, however, that the *Constitutional Draft* was a much longer document than the four short clauses of his paraphrase suggest. Before him Fabri had a handwritten octavo booklet of thirty pages, eight of whose folio sides were, he said, in Hubmaier's hand and the rest written in another hand with his corrections. As Fabri reproduces it, the *Letter of Articles* (with details of the secular ban) presumably comprises the eight sides in Hubmaier's own hand, and the 'other articles', reworked but not composed by him, that is, the *Constitutional Draft*, were spread over the remaining twenty-two sides.[13] It is not hard to imagine what Fabri must have cut out. As a pillar of the Catholic church he was bound to suppress any invocation of God's will in the imminent punishment of the godless, and to play up instead Müntzer's violent and bloodthirsty intentions. The scriptural precepts from which he derived his theology of revolution are entirely lacking, the barrage of biblical citation which studs his writings has been excised. But the echoes that remain are faint, yet audible enough. The demand that the people make an ordinance according to God's will, for instance, harks back to the closing passages of the Eleven Articles of Mühlhausen.[14]

Most striking of all is the exhortation to join a league. Though such an appeal was not unique in the course of the Peasants' War in South-West Germany – it was part and parcel of the treaty of capitulation which Freiburg im Breisgau was forced to sign in May 1525 with the besieging peasant armies under Hans Müller from Bulgenbach, the commander of the Christian Union of the Black Forest[15] – its programmatic emphasis at the outset of the *Constitutional Draft* points indubitably to Müntzer. At most stages therefore, the *Constitutional Draft* betrays unmistakable traces of Müntzer's thought. But what does this tell us? In essence, the 'articles on how to govern' do not go significantly beyond the constitutional blueprint of the Eleven Articles. They set out quite graphically *why* godly rule must be established on earth and they describe in some detail *how* a Christian magistracy shall be installed and a godless regime deposed; but they fail to spell out, even in the broadest of terms, *what* its aims should be. Not even the slogan of the commonweal, hoisted in the Eleven Articles, is invoked. A general commitment to egalitarian Christian communalism can doubtless be inferred from the stipulation that the nobility should receive no special consideration in the election of a new overlord for each region, but that is all.

Müntzer's authorship of the *Constitutional Draft* has indeed been questioned precisely because the fiery spirit of apocalyptic radicalism appears so watered down. Can a man who had come by the end of his Allstedt ministry to regard all worldly lordship as godless be responsible for a blueprint which sets out the conditions for electing new lords?[16] The solution to this apparent paradox lies in Müntzer's understanding of the function and purpose of his Christian leagues. In the leagues he established a *form* or framework in which the elect should act to bring about the transformation of the world, but he steadfastly refused to state what *content* or commitment those leagues should embrace. The configuration of the transformed world, which would restore the order of creation, was, in

Müntzer's eyes, reserved to God's will, not man's. That
is why Müntzer had 'about the Sword and about
tyrants . . . a teaching, but about rulers and government
only an attitude'.[17] What that attitude was emerged in the
Peasants' War in central Germany, when Müntzer at last
fleshed out his political and social vision from the bare
bones of the *Constitutional Draft*.

The consensus of scholarly opinion, therefore, now
agrees that the *Constitutional Draft* contains – in some form
or other – the essence of Müntzer's articles on how to
govern, and attributes the *Letter of Articles* to Hubmaier,[18]
but the relationship between the two has still to be determined. The *Letter of Articles* is itself a misnomer. In the
copy which the Black Forest peasants presented to
Villingen on 8 May 1525 the contents can be divided into
three sections. The document begins with a general exhortation to the council and citizenry of Villingen to join the
rebels' Christian Union in order to put an end to the
oppression and injustice of spiritual and temporal lords
and in their stead uphold the Christian commonweal and
brotherly love, according to a set of articles appended. If
Villingen refused, the rebels continue, it shall be placed
under the secular ban, which is then expounded. The
document closes with a strongly-worded denunciation of
'castles, convents and clerical institutions':

> Whereas all treachery, coercion and depravity befalls
> us and stems from castles, convents and clerical insti-
> tutions, they shall from this hour hence be placed
> under the ban. If, however, nobles, monks or priests
> are willing to quit their castles, convents and foun-
> dations and take up residence in common houses as
> other foreign persons and join this Christian union,
> they shall cordially and righteously be admitted with
> all their goods and chattels. Thereafter everything
> which befits and belongs to them by godly law shall

be accorded to them faithfully and honourably without let or hindrance.[19]

The so-called 'castle article' at the end of the *Letter of Articles* has sometimes been ascribed to Müntzer on account of its militant tone and revolutionary implications, and it certainly finds an echo in his enforced confession and in his dealings with the Thuringian nobility, as well as in the Frankenhausen Articles of the central German rebels in May 1525, in which Müntzer's voice can be heard. How far the 'castle article' in reality contains a call to revolutionary violence may nonetheless be questioned: placing the strongholds of feudal power under the ban may be construed as a friendly warning rather than as the prelude to attack and destruction.[20] In any case, it has now been established that the 'castle article' derives not from Müntzer at all but from the Federal Ordinance (*Bundesordnung*) which the combined Swabian peasant troops drew up at their 'parliament' in Memmingen on 7 March 1525.[21] That ordinance can easily have reached the Saxon and Thuringian rebels, just as did the Twelve Articles of Upper Swabia, since both manifestos were distributed as printed broadsheets. Indeed, the *Bundesordnung*, it has now been demonstrated, itself constitutes the set of appended articles which the peasants submitted to Villingen, since the *Letter of Articles*, despite its name, contains no such set.[22]

Altogether, there is very little in the *Letter of Articles* which can be traced to Müntzer's influence. The *Letter* makes great play of the Christian commonweal (*gemeiner Nutzen*), which Müntzer on occasion contrasts with creaturely selfish interests (*Eigennutz*),[23] but the invocation of the common good is too much a medieval commonplace to be pinned on him alone. The term, in fact, had become the stock-in-trade of late medieval communal opposition movements, without any specifically religious connotations[24] so that it is no surprise to find it cropping up, for instance, in the Eleven Articles of Mühlhausen.[25] Moreover, though there are affinities between Müntzer's and Hubmaier's views on secular authority, in one crucial respect the *Letter of Articles* directly contradicts Müntzer's thinking. The secular ban (regardless of whether it derives from Hubmaier) is not compatible with Müntzer's apocalyptic interpretation of the violent transformation of the world, according to which any form of passive or civil disobedience betrays the fear of man, not the fear of God.[26]

If Müntzer's influence upon Hubmaier was slight, was his impact upon the local peasantry any greater? After the winter of 1524 the South-West German rebels undeniably displayed greater coherence and adamancy. The Klettgauers, who had begun by brushing aside calls to revolt in the autumn, were by January 1525 in open and general rebellion, with God's word and divine justice as their slogans. Furthermore, their captain, Clewi Maier, who hailed from Grießen, the village in which Müntzer is supposed to have lodged, had already led a small detachment the previous December to join the Black Forest rebels under their ideologically militant commander, Hans Müller from Bulgenbach. At the end of January Maier led the Klettgauers on a march to relieve the beleaguered town of Waldshut, Hubmaier's headquarters, in an alliance of solidarity against the Catholic Habsburg authorities.[27] The interpretation of these events, however, is complicated by the difficulty of disentangling Müntzer's possible impact from the spread of radical Zwinglian doctrines throughout the borderland between Switzerland and Germany. Nevertheless, the first signs of radical religious slogans can be detected before Müntzer's arrival in the area. Already on 9 December 1524 Burkhard von Schellenberg, lord of Hüfingen, reported that his subjects were astir with demands for 'nothing but divine law',[28] whilst even before that, in mid-November, the peasants of the Brig valley near Villingen had drawn up a set of articles whose tenor was markedly radical, though they did not expressly invoke divine justice.[29] Such incidents need not surprise us, for the principle of 'divine justice' had an ancient pedigree, stretching well back into the Middle Ages, and had become the rallying-cry of the *Bundschuh* rebellions on the Upper Rhine in the decades just before the Reformation. In the storm years of the Reformation itself the peasants of Swabia and the Upper Rhine harnessed it to the new slogan of the 'holy Gospel' in a potent double-brew of radical religious commitment, which was clearly indebted to Zwingli.[30] The Klettgauers, in particular, took their lead from Zürich between December 1524 and January 1525 in underpinning their secular demands with appeals to divine justice.[31] Müntzer, therefore, may well have encountered the watchwords of godly law or divine justice in South-West Germany, but he hardly inspired them; indeed, the terms are mentioned only twice in his writings.[32]

In the light of this evidence, Müntzer's impact on the South-West German peasants appears astonishingly slight until it is remembered that he remained in correspondence with them after his return to Mühlhausen. Even more significantly, in his confession he revealed that he 'had discussed with the peasants of Klettgau and Hegau near Basel whether they wanted to join forces with him at Mühlhausen and this area [that is, Saxony]. To which they said that if they were paid for it they would come'.[33] What interpretation to place upon that undertaking is by no means straightforward. The Upper German and Swiss villages were a major recruiting-ground for mercenaries, whose loyalties were notoriously fickle. It may be wise to draw a distinction, therefore, between Müntzer's hopes and the peasants' promises. Müntzer made a mark in South-West Germany: of that there can be no doubt. But he was an interloper, on the run, unable to preach freely (in a Saxon dialect which must have bemused his Alemannic audience) – and, above all, he was in local competition with eminent and established theologians, not merely Zwingli, but the unquestionably radical and militant Hubmaier as well, the fate of whose religious reforms in Waldshut was inextricably bound up with the progress of the peasants' insurrection. Sometime in the New Year of 1525 Müntzer headed home, as much influenced as influencing.

On the journey to Saxony Müntzer was imprisoned briefly in Fulda in eastern Hessen, where rioting took place at the beginning of February over the introduction of evangelical preaching. There is no reason to think that Müntzer had a hand in instigating the anticlerical protests – more likely he was caught up in the commotion by chance – but if he had known the identity of his prisoner, the abbot of Fulda afterwards declared, he would never have released him. By late February Müntzer was back in Mühlhausen and within a few days was installed by popular acclaim as rector of St Mary's, the largest church in the city. That he was able to return to an official post is striking testimony to the transformation in civic affairs which had occurred during his absence.

Before Christmas Pfeiffer had scoured Mühlhausen's villages to drum up support for his readmittance. On his urging, a group of peasants in full array marched on the suburbs, where Pfeiffer delivered a fiery and defiant sermon. In panic, the council called the citizenry to arms and shut the city gates, but part of the commons defied its instructions and rallied to the insurgents at the Felchta gate. The council's hold on the citizenry was so shaky that it could not prevent Pfeiffer's reinstatement at St Nicholas, and had to pledge to refer all business to the

commons for approval. Truly, as Hans Zeiß reported to
Georg Spalatin some weeks later, 'the word has been
taken from it [the council] and strange things are afoot'.[34]
Pfeiffer's ability to retrieve a situation so recently forlorn
is indeed remarkable, the more so given the attitude in
September of Mühlhausen's villages to the overtures of
the radicals and the Eleven Articles. His success should
clearly be attributed to hard graft and groundwork in the
countryside, listening and responding to the peasants'
grievances – they were not, after all, averse to the new
religious doctrines – which secured him a following that
was to remain loyal throughout the Peasants' War. The
council, for its part, which had been able to tap sufficient
collective instincts of self-preservation in September to
have Müntzer and Pfeiffer expelled, fell victim to the
unusually fluid and permeable constitution which the
Recess of 1523 had bequeathed. The balance of power
between council and committee of Eight was inherently
unstable and could easily be capsized by subversion from
within, just as occurred ten years later in the prelude
to the Anabaptist kingdom of Zion in Münster.[35] What
provided the immediate pretext for political agitation was
the failure of the civic authorities, caught between Catholic patricians and propertied craftsmen sympathetic to
reform – to commit themselves wholeheartedly to the
introduction of evangelical worship. Despite the anticlerical outbursts of the preceding two years Mühlhausen
was in name still a Catholic city, though evangelical
preachers were active in several of its churches.

    With Pfeiffer's reappearance the work of reform could
at last begin in earnest. In the first week of January 1525
Catholic altarpieces were removed from churches and
convents; in St Blasius's a new altar table was placed in
front of the choir to mark the new liturgical function of
holy communion. The Dominican and Franciscan friaries
were attacked, images smashed, their inmates driven out,

property seized and the houses dissolved. The council managed to prevent the mob from plundering the city's third convent of St Mary Magdalen, which housed a community of penitent nuns, only to remove the jewelry and precious objects itself to the town hall, and to bar the nuns from celebrating Catholic rites in their church. The sacking of the Dominican convent had ominous consequences, for the friars called immediately upon the city's princely neighbours, duke George of Saxony and landgrave Philip of Hessen, to help restitute their property. The princes were likewise approached by the two disgraced mayors, Rodemann and Wettich, with a plea for reinstatement. Intervention by the powerful territorial rulers on its doorstep was what Mühlhausen feared most of all, and it could expect little assistance from its protectors, the ernestine Saxon princes. The situation, therefore, that confronted Müntzer on his return was both precarious and volatile, not only for the council but for the city as a whole.

Müntzer, characteristically, was encouraged, not deterred. His installation as preacher at St Mary's came about, it seems, without the council's knowledge or consent, on the insistence of three suburban parishes, St Nicholas, St Peter and St George. With the eviction of the previous collators of the benefice, the Knights of the Teutonic Order, Müntzer handsomely took up residence in their spacious quarters. From the pulpit Müntzer praised the signs of a purified community: the removal of idols from the churches and the preaching of the unadulterated Gospel. But to gain salvation, he warned his congregation, they must now remove the idols from their own homes as well, fine tableware and jewelry, silverware and coin: 'so long as you love these, the spirit of God will not dwell in you.'[36] It is damning evidence for Müntzer's growing estrangement from reality that, far from being joyously received as the harbinger of redemption, this

message elicited no reponse whatsoever from his
audience.

That Müntzer could not count upon unqualified or
unquestioning allegiance from the commons of
Mühlhausen was further underscored by a muster of the
citizenry carried out on 9 March. Though Sittich von
Berlepsch, whose informers reported on the event,
declared that Müntzer and Pfeiffer had called the muster
to test the militia's readiness in the face of external danger,
it seems constitutionally improbable that anyone bar the
council could have issued the necessary authority. The
muster, which took place in open countryside just north
of the city on the way to Ammern, amounted to a full-
scale mobilisation; around two thousand men from the
city and its villages were on parade, together with their
fire-arms and field artillery (both stuffed with paper!). In
their midst Müntzer mounted a horse and harangued the
assembled company from the saddle. 'Render unto Caesar
the things that are Caesar's', the report went, 'and come
to a proper accord with monks and priests, as the imperial
government has instructed you.' Then a more authentic
note was stuck. 'Dear Christian brothers, the word of God
must undergo tribulation. You know and see that I have
suffered much adversity on account of God's word which
I preach to you – so that the Emperor and many princes
would gladly take it away from you. But they cannot –
they will shortly be driven out themselves by their own
subjects. Whosoever among you is prepared to stand by
God's word even unto death, and testify on oath to it, let
him raise a finger; those who will not, let them step aside.'
His flow was interrupted by the captain of the militia,
Eberhard von Bodungen, who exclaimed in exasperation:
'Dear citizens, have you not already had your fill of oaths
by the basketful, enough to hang round your necks?'
Preaching, he declared, belonged in church, not in the
countryside. With that the company grew restive, refused

to swear an oath, and marched back to Mühlhausen in disgust, where they demanded barrels of beer for their exertions. When those were drunk dry, one of the councillors, himself clearly the worse for wear, called for replenishments and led a gang of tipsy hotheads to St Mary Magdalen, where they set upon the nunnery, so recently spared from plunder, drove out the few remaining sisters, smashed everything in sight, tore down and burnt what images they could find, and carried off a cask of ale to the suburb of St Nicholas.[37]

These scenes of debauched and mindless vandalism cannot conceal that Müntzer's bluff had been well and truly called. For his intentions at the muster must surely be read as a deliberate attempt to chivvy the citizens into swearing allegiance to a new Christian league.[38] But Mühlhausen was not Allstedt: Müntzer was no longer the guiding light of a small community, moulded in his image, but one religious radical amongst others, struggling to assert the primacy of his vision in a much larger commune which he could not manipulate at will. What influence he was able to exert seems, moreover, to have depended on support from Pfeiffer and his suburban following, though relations between the two men are so shadowy that considerable disagreement persists about their common purpose. During March the two preachers acted in concert to put pressure on the council to undertake a radical recasting of municipal affairs, in which, so rumour had it, Müntzer was to become city secretary and Pfeiffer city treasurer.[39] Here at last is evidence – albeit unreliable – that Müntzer had left the Eleven Articles behind and was contemplating some form of civic theocracy. After three days' fruitless negotiations in All Saints church over the installation of a new council the citizens at large were summoned to Müntzer's own much larger church of St Mary's on 16 March, where, according to the Mühlhausen chronicle, it was Pfeiffer, rather than

Müntzer, who took the lead in addressing the assembled multitude. The old council, he declared, had agreed to stand down in favour of new elections. 'Not at all', one of the mayors was stung to reply, 'the council did not agree, but said that if the commons so wished, we must acquiesce.' Thereupon a vote was taken, with each man being asked his opinion in turn. Once the four tellers had collected the votes Pfeiffer again mounted the pulpit to announce the result: a majority of three to one in favour of a new council. The votes cast – 660 for, 204 against[40] – confirm the resounding margin of victory, though less than half the number of eligible electors appears to have participated. In any case, the chronicle sourly remarked, the majority was swollen by intimidation and cajolery.

The formal deposition of the old council took place the next day at the town hall. In its stead a new, so-called Eternal Council, comprising sixteen members, was appointed, which prompted the city syndic, Dr Johann von Otthera, to exclaim: 'He has cast down the mighty from their seats, and has exalted them of low degree. What a wondrous God is he!' But despite its designation as 'Eternal', a term which deliberately echoed the Eleven Articles, the new council failed to live up to the lofty expectations vested in it – nor did it admit the two preachers to its counsels. Under its regime, it is true, the Mass was abolished during Holy Week and replaced by a service of commemoration in which the sacraments were no longer to be administered bodily, but 'received in each believer's heart'. With that, the last vestiges of Catholicism were finally swept aside and the seal was set on Mühlhausen's formal conversion into a Protestant city of spiritualist observance. On the Eternal Council's instructions, moreover, a sheep farm belonging to the Teutonic Order at Pfaffenrode was expropriated, though whether that should be regarded as the first step towards a 'revolutionary destruction of feudal property' is more than doubtful.[41] Beyond these measures, however, the council did not venture, for its composition was too diverse and broadly based to serve as the instrument of a revolutionary programme. Its sixteen members were drawn from previous councillors, the committee of Eight and representatives of the city wards: a cross-section of the populace both by wealth and occupation, rather than the tightly knit group of radicals upon whom Müntzer pinned his hopes.[42]

Out of chagrin, it appears, Müntzer reverted to the formation of a covenanted band of the elect along the lines of his Allstedt leagues. Reporting to duke George on 17 April 1525 Sittich von Berlepsch concluded: 'The Allstedter has had a white pennant made from thirty ells of coarse silk, on which has been painted a rainbow with the words *verbum domini manet in aeternum* and a verse stating "this is the emblem of the Eternal League of God: let all those who will stand by the league assemble hereunder" '. This banner Müntzer then placed by the pulpit in St Mary's in a pointed jibe at the Eternal Council whose election had taken place there. In contrast to his broad defensive alliance in Allstedt, however, which had embraced both godly and godless, Müntzer saw his Mühlhausen league from the outset as an Old Testament covenant between God and the vanguard of true believers who were in the words of Daniel ch. 7, v. 27 'the people of the saints of the most High, whose kingdom is an everlasting kingdom'. Its organisation was openly military, with captain, ensign, sergeants, corporals, piper, drummer, quartermaster, field-surgeon, clerk and chaplain.[43] No names are entered against these posts in the surviving register, except for Pfeiffer as chaplain. His role is further underscored by the testimony of one rich member of the league, the draper Claus Haldecke, who also sat on the Eternal Council, that the league had been enrolled outside the Felchta gate, the headquarters of

Pfeiffer's agitation in St Nicholas, and at some remove from Müntzer's inner-city parish of St Mary's. To the 219 recorded names in the one surviving list (itself a copy and impossible to date accurately) may with certainty be added another thirty or so from other sources,[44] though Müntzer's name, strikingly enough, is nowhere mentioned. At the beginning the league was drawn more conspicuously from the poorer and plebeian elements of the city and its suburbs,[45] but Müntzer announced that he intended to recruit a further two thousand men from the surrounding countryside.

The military character of the Eternal League and its composition of activists leave no doubt that, for Müntzer, the battle against the godless was at hand. Throughout March and April 1525 the peasant unrest which had been smouldering in South-West Germany at last burst into open rebellion, spreading rapidly northeastwards through Franconia and Hessen to the fringes of Thuringia. Convinced that the day of judgement was nigh, Müntzer threw his energies into rousing the common people to take up arms in the name of the Lord. Sittich von Berlepsch, an astute and well-informed observer of the situation, was convinced that the Harz, Hainich and Hainleite, Müntzer's native district around Nordhausen, would fall to the rebels' cause if the agitation in Mühlhausen did not cease. In Nordhausen itself a party of radicals, led by two men only recently arrived from Mühlhausen, was clamouring for the installation of an Eternal Council.[46] Whether they were active henchmen of Müntzer is unclear, but he had certainly kept in touch with his followers in Allstedt, whose spirits he sought to raise by declaring

The false prophets will have to go swimming soon enough with their Nimrod [the Saxon princes], but you can still be certain of escaping that sort of pleasure bath. If you are willing to recognise your fall, you can certainly still be helped.[47]

South of Mühlhausen, too, Berlepsch's headquarters of Langensalza harboured many followers who had attended Müntzer's sermons in the nearby city, whilst preachers sympathetic to his vision such as Melchior Rinck, Heinrich Fuchs, Hans Hut and Hans Römer were active to the south-west in the forest of Eisenach on the borders of Thuringia. There the formation of a peasant troop in the Upper Werra valley signalled the onset of open rebellion, which was rapidly followed by a general rising in northern Thuringia and an urban revolt in Langensalza at the end of April, to which Pfeiffer and the popular movement in Mühlhausen immediately offered their support, only to have it declined.[48] For Müntzer, the revolt in Langensalza was the sign that his apocalyptic struggle had entered its decisive stage.

This chain of events put Mühlhausen's princely neighbours onto active alert. At a meeting in Naumburg on 11/12 April Protestant and Catholic officials from Hessen, and electoral and ducal Saxony, had already closed ranks in a joint strategy of suppression. Luther, for his part, watched the rampant revolt with mounting alarm. The Swabian peasants had appealed to him and other leading reformers to adjudicate upon their demand for divine justice. In response Luther composed his *Admonition to Peace: A Reply to the Twelve Articles of the Peasants in Swabia*, in which he evinced some sympathy for the rebels' demands but insisted that violence could never be justified to rectify their grievances. But the *Admonition* does not give the princes *carte blanche*: on the contrary, Luther takes them to task for giving grounds for rebellion:

We have no one on earth to thank for this disastrous
rebellion, except you princes and lords, and
especially you blind bishops and mad priests and
monks, whose hearts are hardened, even to the
present day. You do not cease to rant and rave
against the holy gospel, even though you know that
it is true and that you cannot refute it. In addition,
as temporal rulers you do nothing but cheat and rob
the people so that you may lead a life of luxury and
extravagance. The poor common people cannot bear
it any longer. The sword is already at your throats,
but you think that you can sit so firm in the saddle
that no one can unhorse you.

Luther's eschatological fears ring out in warning:

Since you are the cause of this wrath of God, it will
undoubtedly come upon you, unless you mend your
ways in time. The signs in heaven and the wonders
on earth are meant for you, dear lords. . . . A great
part of God's wrath has already come, for God is
sending many false teachers and prophets among us,
so that through our error and blasphemy we may
richly deserve hell and everlasting damnation. . . .
You must become different men and yield to God's
word. If you do not do this amicably and willingly,
then you will be compelled to do it by force and
destruction. If these peasants do not compel you,
others will.[49]

Though the attack on false prophets merely reiterated the
denunciation of Müntzer a year earlier in the *Letter to the
Princes of Saxony concerning the Rebellious Spirit*, Luther's
language and argument in the first part of the *Admonition*
sound an uncanny echo of Müntzer's own condemnation
of the princes. If in their understanding of faith the two

reformers had grown poles part, in their understanding
of history – God's righteousness in the world – they
remained closer to each other than either cared to
acknowledge. That his own princes should be obliged to
combine with duke George, the arch-Catholic foe, was
indeed bitter gall to Luther, who railed at them for failing
to comprehend his teaching: 'You did not want to know
what I taught or what the gospel is; now the one who
will soon teach you is at the door, unless you change
your ways.' Luther did not exculpate the peasantry for
resorting to violence; rather, he flung his energies into
weaning them away from seditious preachers. Already on
24 April a peasant from Rietnorthausen near Sangerhausen had challenged Müntzer in St Mary's over his
doctrine of the Spirit; citing the vision of Cornelius the
centurion in Acts ch. 10 he enquired whether all believers
in Christ had received the Holy Spirit at that time. It is
hard to avoid the conclusion that the unnamed peasant
was a Lutheran *agent provocateur* – he was sufficiently well
briefed to sustain a disputation with Müntzer, who could
spout Scripture at will, for four hours, with some of the
congregation taking his side, until in the end he was run
out of town by Müntzer's activists, who barely let him
escape with his life.[50]

During the last days of April Luther bestirred himself
from his comfortable headquarters in Wittenberg to
undertake a strenuous preaching tour in western
Saxony.[51] Although he did not approach Mühlhausen
itself, he is known to have delivered sermons in Stolberg
(Müntzer's birthplace), Nordhausen (where he was
heckled), and Wallhausen by Sangerhausen, within
hailing distance of Allstedt. On 1 May Hans Zeiß, the
Saxon official there, reported that Luther was touring the
county of Mansfeld, but could not prevent the peasantry
rallying to arms. That his efforts had availed nothing
Luther himself acknowledged on his return home, where

he bitterly exclaimed: 'I have seen with my own eyes a hundred thousand devils lurking in one man.' Faced with his humiliating failure Luther's mood turned to blackest savagery as he took up his pen once more to scarify the 'other' peasants (that is, the Saxon and Thuringian rebels) who were committing bloodshed on his doorstep. *Against the Robbing and Murdering Hordes of Peasants*, written when the conflagration was almost over, is indeed a terrible document, a testimony to the deepest mortification, but although Luther now exhorted the princes to cut down the peasants without mercy, he did not lose sight of the real culprit, Müntzer, 'that archdevil who rules at Mühlhausen, and does nothing except stir up robbery, murder and bloodshed'.[52] But Luther's judgement was clouded by hatred. Müntzer's role in the Peasants' War in central Germany was neither so dominant, nor his leadership so undisputed, his support neither so unswerving, nor his aims so unequivocally shared as the subsequent historiographical legend has asserted.

Much of that legend was originally inspired by Luther himself, who seized upon several of Müntzer's letters at the height of hostilities to illustrate *A Shocking History and God's Judgement on Thomas Müntzer*, published shortly after Müntzer's capture in May 1525 with the purpose of disqualifying and anathematising his beliefs.[53] Foremost amongst these letters was the appeal which Müntzer addressed to his followers in Allstedt around 26/27 April, on hearing the news from Langensalza and of the rising in the Eichsfeld. The letter demonstrates the solidarity and commitment upon which Müntzer still counted amongst his former associates: indeed, the members of his Allstedt leagues were the only group of followers who fought *en masse* with Müntzer to the bitter end. With its blazing apocalyptic imagery the appeal sloughs off the contortions and obscurities of his tracts, sagging under the weight of biblical allusion. In its immediacy and vividness it surely conveys something of the spellbinding quality of his pulpit oratory.

> How long are you going to slumber, how long are you going to resist God's will. . . . I tell you this, that if you are unwilling to suffer for the sake of God, then you will have to be martyrs for the devil. . . . The whole of Germany, France, Italy is awake; the master wants to set the game in motion, the evil-doers are for it. At Fulda four abbeys were laid waste during Easter week, the peasants in the Klettgau and the Hegau in the Black Forest have risen, three thousand strong, and the size of the peasant host is growing all the time.[54]

Müntzer's reassuring words the previous month give way to a blatant call to extirpate the godless:

> Even if there are only three of you whose trust in God is unperturbable and who seek his name and honour alone, you need have no fear of a hundred thousand. So go to it, go to it, go to it! The time has come, the evil-doers are running like scared dogs! Alert the brothers, so that they may be at peace, and testify to their conversion. It is absolutely crucial – absolutely necessary! Go to it, go to it, go to it! Show no pity, even though Esau suggest kind words to you, Genesis 33. Pay no attention to the cries of the godless. They will entreat you ever so warmly, they will whimper and wheedle like children. Show no pity, as God has commanded in the words of Moses, Deuteronomy 7; and he has revealed the same thing to us too. Alert the villages and towns and especially the mineworkers and other good fellows who will be of use. We cannot slumber any longer.[55]

Müntzer spells out his message to the leaders of his Allstedt leagues, Balthasar Stübner, Barthel and Valentin Krump, and Bischoff from Wolferode:

> Let this letter go on to the miners. My printer is coming in the next few days. . . . There is nothing else I can do at the moment, or I would instruct the brothers so thoroughly that their heart would be much larger than all the castles and weapons of the godless evil-doers throughout the world. Go to it, go to it, while the fire is hot! Don't let your sword grow cold, don't let it hang down limply! Hammer away ding-dong on the anvils of Nimrod, cast down their tower to the ground! As long as they live it is impossible for you to rid yourselves of the fear of men. One cannot say anything to you about God as long as they rule over you. Go to it, go to it, while it is day! God goes before you; follow, follow! . . . [56]

But Müntzer tempered his 'Coraggio!' with a caution:

> So do not be deterred. God is with you, as is written in 2 Chronicles. This is what God says, 'You should have no fear. You should not shrink from this great host: it is not your fight, but the Lord's.'[57]

With that, the 'servant of God against the godless', as Müntzer signed himself, served notice on his followers that theirs was not a creaturely struggle for the betterment of their worldly lot, but a transcendent battle in the name of God, a holy war against the reprobate and obdurate.

Fired with this spirit, Müntzer and Pfeiffer set out together for Langensalza on 26 April under the banner of the Eternal League with around four hundred followers, on hearing that the Catholic Saxon official, Sittich von Berlepsch, had imprisoned three dissidents and was threatening to kill them. Müntzer's anger at Berlepsch emerged later in statements by local peasants to whom he wrote that 'they should keep a close watch for the administrator, for the tyrant, the bloodhound, so that he did not escape from Salza, for things would not go well if he got out of Salza; he should be struck dead'.[58] On arrival, however, the Mühlhausen contingent found that calm had been restored. After the citizens had thanked them with two barrels of beer, the contingent withdrew to Höngeda, where it pitched camp for the night. The next day, instead of disbanding, Müntzer led part of the contingent to sack the abbey of Volkenroda, east of Mühlhausen, where they smashed images and burnt rent-books and estate records. Pfeiffer, meanwhile, withdrew to Mühlhausen to rally support for the gathering rebellion.

An urban contingent under the two preachers, apparently backed by the Eternal Council, then joined forces with the peasants at Görmar to form a combined Mühlhausen-Thuringian army, whose first aim was to link up with the north Thuringian rebels encamped at Frankenhausen, who had sent an urgent request for two hundred reinforcements. On 29 April, full of righteous certainty, Müntzer promised them unlimited support, assuring them of victory if they would trust in God alone:

We reply that we will not send a small band like that to you but rather that everyone, everyone, as many as we have, wants to come to you, marching through all the countryside. . . . You need fear no one. The voice of the Lord says: Look, the strength of my needy people will be increased, who will dare attack them? So be bold and put your trust in God alone, and he will endow your small band with more strength than you would ever believe. . . . But do see that no fine words persuade you to show a fraudulent clemency, and your cause will surely prevail.[59]

The bold commitment to God's cause was rapidly belied by the behaviour of the army. The previous day a detachment of irregulars ransacked St Mary Magdalen's nunnery and the estate of Rudolf von Hopfgarten in Schlotheim, carrying off what they could find to the camp at Görmar; there the booty – plate and jewels, not provisions – was divided amongst the troops by Müntzer's own hand after a sermon, seemingly quite blind to the danger of pandering to creaturely desires.

Moreover, when the army reached Ebeleben on 29 April, its purpose faltered. A party of insurgents from the Eichsfeld had already turned up at Görmar laden with plunder, and the arrival of a further seven hundred men at Ebeleben plunged the rebels into deep confusion over the correct strategy. The Eichsfeld captains – on their knees, in one account – pleaded with Müntzer, Pfeiffer and the field commanders to divert to the Eichsfeld, where the lords had counteradvanced as far as Dingelstädt. For Müntzer, with his eyes set firmly on his native territory and a reckoning with count Ernst von Mansfeld, the call to change direction was bound to mean a crucial waste of time and effort, not least since he had just vouchsafed unqualified assistance to the rebels at Frankenhausen. But Pfeiffer, mindful of the support which he had recruited in the Eichsfeld as the prelude to his return to Mühlhausen the previous December, urged the troops to rescue the Eichsfeld peasantry in its extremity. After considerable debate, Pfeiffer's voice carried the day, and the army duly headed westwards. The week-long campaign of plunder and destruction at the beginning of May, during which scores of castles and convents were sacked and their inmates put to flight, was indeed a fateful turning-point in the Thuringian revolt, for it tied up the

Mühlhausen-Thuringian army in the west just when the rest of Thuringia and western Saxony was being engulfed by mass rebellion.

The predicament at Ebeleben has been often construed as an ideological rift between Müntzer, the champion of a general vision of Christian liberation, and Pfeiffer, the advocate of violent but local initiatives against the feudal hierarchy.[60] In fact, the sources, though plentiful enough, are much too contradictory to determine how the debate within the army went.[61] Tactical ignorance and uncertainty, rather than an ideological split, may have been responsible for the confusion. The final decision should have lain with the field commanders, but according to Zeiß, Müntzer and Pfeiffer had usurped their function.[62] It is certainly worth noting that Claus Rautenzweig's confession (one of the Allstedt league members) recalled a decision to split the army in two, with one part making for Frankenhausen and the other turning to the Eichsfeld.[63] There were certainly divisions within the rebels' camp, but there is no convincing evidence that Müntzer and Pfeiffer were seriously at odds over the ultimate strategy, which was to march northeastwards and link up with the Frankenhausen army; Pfeiffer's own confession, after all, speaks of their intention to bring count Ernst von Mansfeld to his knees.[64]

In any case, the Eichsfeld campaign was not altogether a strategic blunder. In the camp at Ebeleben two Thuringian nobles, count Günther von Schwarzburg and count Ernst von Hohnstein, had – clearly under duress – joined Müntzer's covenanted band as common brothers, and in the course of the Eichsfeld expedition a further four local lords were pressed into membership on terms identical with the 'castle article' of the Federal Ordinance (*Bundesordnung*) of Upper Swabia.[65] As Müntzer proudly reported to count Günther on 4 May from Duderstadt:

Your brothers, Kurt von Dittichenrode, Heinrich Hake, Christopher von Altendorf and Balthasar von Bendeleben have been received into our covenant, and we have promised them Christian freedom from any molestation or unfair impositions and I have given them a letter of safe-conduct in my own hand, providing it transpires that they do not hinder the righteousness of God or persecute the preachers.[66]

Since these measures served to neutralise the Thuringian nobility at the height of the conflict – in the end the entire countship of the region, the implacable Ernst von Mansfeld apart, succumbed to offers of protective alliance – their military value should not be underestimated. The Thuringian insurgents, moreover, never again had such success as in their offensive in the Eichsfeld: the seizure of booty and the example of deterrence should not be underrated.

At the end of the campaign a detachment of rebels headed straight for Frankenhausen, but the bulk of the Mühlhausen-Thuringian troop under the two preachers made its way back to the imperial city, despite the worsening situation of the main rebel army. On 6 May the peasants from Sangerhausen, north of Allstedt, long-standing adherents of Müntzer, proudly announced that they had formed a godly league:

We poor country folk from the villages of the whole district of Sangerhausen want you to know that we country folk, together with the town of Sanger-hausen, the council and the bailiff, have vowed and sworn a divine covenant, in the love of God and the holy gospel, being ready to offer up our bodies and lives for it.[67]

Their appeal for immediate assistance was echoed the
next day by the Frankenhausen army itself, which warned
Mühlhausen in desperation that there was no hope of
withstanding duke George or Ernst von Mansfeld
'without your help and support and that of God'. The
rebels bluntly called on the city to make good its recent
promise of reinforcements: 'Unless you do so our Christian blood will be shed in great quantities, which will be
a great scandal and detrimental to the holy gospel, since
we would never have presumed to act without the help
of God and yourselves.'[68] Yet notwithstanding their
extremity Müntzer waited until 10 May to set out for
Frankenhausen with a mere three hundred followers –
barely a sixth of the militia mustered on 9 March! –
arriving at the camp at noon two days later.

This extraordinary delay has never satisfactorily been
explained. Strategic incompetence and overvaulting
confidence may be partly to blame. On 7 May, for
instance, Müntzer could write to the rebels of Schmalkalden, at the furthermost point of southwestern
Thuringia, promising imminent support, at the very time
when he was trying to rouse the citizens of Mühlhausen
to march in quite the opposite direction northeastwards
towards Frankenhausen. In his reassurance to Schmalkalden, however, Müntzer makes no bones about his
exasperation at the attitude of the local populace:

We want to do everything in our power to assist you.
Just be patient for a short while with our brothers,
for it is proving extraordinarily hard work to lick
them into shape, for they are much coarser people
than anyone could conceive. For in many respects
you have become conscious of what it is that
oppresses you, while we are not able to make our
folk here aware of this in any wholehearted way; but

because God is driving them forcibly we simply have to work with them.[69]

That enthusiasm for the rebels' cause was far from universal in Mühlhausen emerged with telling clarity on 8 May in Müntzer's note to the council:

> Satan has an extraordinary amount to do; he would like to thwart the common good and does so through his own vessel, and it is highly desirable that those creating such disruption should first be summoned before today's circle [the army's 'ring of justice'] and threatened with the direst consequences to prevent them harming your interests as magistrates and those of the city as a whole. But if they will not comply with this, then they should be punished by the authority of the host.[70]

The sudden loss of nerve within a city whose inhabitants had actively and successfully participated in the rebellion is indeed puzzling. The Eternal Council's subsequent disclaimer (contained in Müntzer's confession) that it had not publicly endorsed Mühlhausen's involvement, only tacitly tolerated it, may well be true, but the thrust of Müntzer's message suggests that the trouble lay elsewhere. Did it derive from a split between Müntzer and Pfeiffer? The former's mention of Satan's 'vessel' and his warning to the council that 'whenever Judas comes to light, his fate is already sealed' used to be taken as strong indication that the two preachers had fallen out over a common course of action: the decision at Ebeleben a week earlier had only papered over irreconcilable differences between a 'moderate' and a 'radical' wing, the followers of the local rebel Pfeiffer and those committed to the visionary revolutionary Müntzer.[71] The only direct evidence which might confirm this suspicion stems from

Müntzer's alleged pleasure after the defeat at Franken-hausen on hearing of Pfeiffer's arrest near Eisenach.[72] Against that must be set not only Pfeiffer's own (admit-tedly brief) testimony, in which his declared intentions – the extirpation of godless authority and the introduction of a Christian Reformation – betray no obvious deviation from Müntzer's,[73] and the statement of Pfeiffer's brother, Georg Schwertfeger, that he knew of no difference in aims and opinion between the two men.[74] Now that a perfectly plausible tactical explanation for Pfeiffer's decision to stay behind in Mühlhausen has been given,[75] namely to guard their strategic headquarters, the case for a breach in prin-ciple between the two preachers remains not proven.

Despite the chafing delay in Mühlhausen, Müntzer's ultimate resolve was not in question. The apocalyptic language of the *Magnificat* courses through his final corre-spondence. Power shall be given to the common people; the mighty cast down; the lowly exalted; the 'treacherous, traitorous biblical scholars' at last confounded – all these injunctions in his stern reproof to Eisenach on 9 May for impeding the rebels' cause, a letter signed with a new flourish 'Thomas Müntzer, with the sword of Gideon'. The example of the prophets Daniel, Elijah or John the Baptist he now cast aside in favour of Gideon, the man of action, who with his small band of Israelites smote the mighty hordes of the Midianites.

But Müntzer's delayed departure had already plunged the main Thuringian army into turmoil and despondency and squandered the strategic advantage which Franken-hausen had gained during the first week of May. The general rising had begun with a civic revolt in Franken-hausen at the end of April against its lords, the counts of Schwarzburg. At first the rebels' demands were directed solely towards sweeping changes in municipal govern-ment, but within a week Frankenhausen had become the focus of mass rebellion in town and country, as seven

thousand peasants and townfolk from Allstedt, Sangerhausen, Stolberg, the Mansfeld, Schwarzburg and albertine Saxon territories flocked to the town to form a united
army, the Frankenhausen troop. Thereupon the rebels
presented the counts of Stolberg and Schwarzburg with
their demands under four headings.

1. Free and unadulterated preaching of the Gospel;
2. Free usufruct of forest, water, pasture, and rights of
    chase;
3. Destruction of excessive nobles' castles, and distri-
    bution of their provisions amongst the army;
4. Abandonment of noble titles in favour of God's
    honour alone. Thereafter restitution of nobles' prop-
    erty and receipt of expropriated monastic estates
    within their jurisdictions, save for provisions, again to
    be shared amongst the common man. Any mortgaged
    lands likewise to be restored to the lords.[76]

Though this programme does not survive as an original
list of articles, it evidently represents a composite of ideas.
The first two demands can be traced directly to the Twelve
Articles of Upper Swabia; the third article, by contrast,
echoes the 'castle article' in the *Letter of Articles*, deriving
from the Federal Ordinance of Upper Swabia, in the more
radical twist lent it by Pfeiffer, namely that in each district
only one castle should be left standing and the remainder
razed to the ground.[77] Only in the fourth article is
Müntzer's influence at all palpable; 'all glory, fame and
honour, all dignity and splendour and acclamation be
given to you alone, eternal son of God' marks the opening
sentence of the *Vindication and Refutation*, whilst the
provision for reinstating lords if they uphold the Gospel
is contained in his confession and, obliquely, in the *Constitutional Draft*.

The adoption of these demands, however, did not

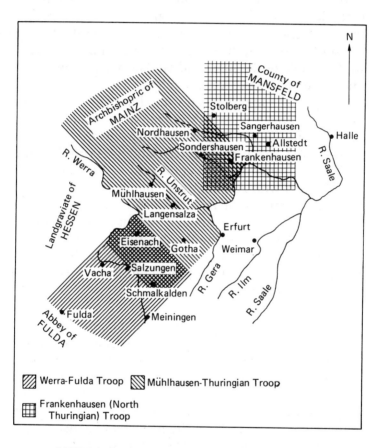

N

Archbishopric of MAINZ

County of MANSFELD

Stolberg

Sangerhausen

Nordhausen

Allstedt

Halle

Sondershausen

Frankenhausen

R. Werra

R. Unstrut

R. Saale

Mühlhausen

Langensalza

Landgraviate of HESSEN

Erfurt

Eisenach

Gotha

Weimar

Vacha

Salzungen

R. Gera

R. Ilm

Schmalkalden

R. Saale

Fulda

Meiningen

Abbey of FULDA

Werra-Fulda Troop   Mühlhausen-Thuringian Troop

Frankenhausen (North Thuringian) Troop

MAP 8   The Peasants' War in Central Germany

herald any decisive action. Though the Frankenhausen army mounted several limited expeditions in the immediate neighbourhood, it was clearly pinning its hopes on the arrival of the Mühlhausen contingent before embarking on a major campaign. Once the armies had joined forces they planned to head northwards to Sangerhausen, whose capture would have opened the gateway to the whole of the Mansfeld lands,[78] where the peasants and miners were expected to rally to a general Thuringian uprising. But Sangerhausen waited in vain for the armies to appear. By the time Müntzer and his Mühlhausen detachment has reached Frankenhausen, the princes had crushed the revolt in southern and western Thuringia, whilst the Frankenhausen commanders had begun peace negotiations with Albrecht von Mansfeld.

At the camp Müntzer at once took charge of affairs, though the military command remained with Bonaventura Kürschner from Frankenhausen.[79] The conciliatory overtures of count Albrecht, a staunch Lutheran unlike his arch-Catholic brother Ernst, Müntzer brushed aside with contempt:

Couldn't you find in your Lutheran pudding and your Wittenberg soup what Ezekiel has prophesied in his thirty-seventh chapter? You haven't even been able to detect the flavour, because of that Martinian peasant filth of yours, of what the same prophet goes on to say in the thirty-ninth chapter, that God instructs all the birds of the heavens to consume the flesh of the princes. . . . Do you imagine that God is less concerned about his people than he is about you tyrants?[80]

Writing the same day to his bogey, Ernst von Mansfeld, Müntzer stooped to sheer abuse: 'Just tell us, you miserable, wretched sack of worms, who made you a prince over the people whom God redeemed with his dear blood?' Should he refuse to humble himself and repent, Müntzer was ready with an ultimatum:

> We want your answer this very evening; otherwise we will descend on you in the name of the God of hosts; so you know what to expect. We shall execute without delay what God has commanded us; so do your best, too. I'm on my way.[81]

Such braggadocio bore no relation whatever to the military strength of the Frankenhausen army, whose puny artillery had no chance of storming Ernst's stronghold of Heldrungen castle, a few miles to the south. Nor could it conceal that much of Thuringia had failed to rally to the peasants' cause. In extremity Müntzer sent a string of vain appeals for reinforcements to Ehrich, Walkenried and Erfurt, which had itself been seized by civic revolt a week earlier.[82]

The army was effectively marooned in Frankenhausen; no further sorties were mounted in the surrounding district. It was almost as if the peasants were waiting for the princes' onslaught. Müntzer bestrode the camp as the executor of God's law. With his full assent three of Ernst von Mansfeld's servants, Matern von Gehofen, Georg Buchner, and the priest Steffan Hartenstein, were executed 'in the fear of God' in the name of revolutionary justice after the count had refused to appear before the rebels' tribunal.[83] On 14 May a small contingent of Hessians and Brunswickers was beaten off at the foot of the hill outside Frankenhausen – 'Battle Hill', as it came to be known – where the rebels had taken up position. They then closed ranks by withdrawing to the flat summit of the hill and marshalling their carts and cannon into a laager. Overnight they waited, watchful and in prayer. In the morning the full horror of their predicament dawned

upon the rebels. What seemed a stronghold was in truth
a trap.[84] As duke George of Saxony's troops approached
to join forces with the Hessian and Brunswick cavalry,
the peasants issued a desperate appeal for mercy:

> We confess Christ. We are not here to harm anyone,
> John 2, but to see that divine justice is maintained.
> We are not here to shed blood, either. If your aims
> are the same, then we have no desire to harm you.
> Everyone should be guided by that.[85]

Back came the poisoned bait:

> If you turn over to us, alive, the false prophet
> Thomas Müntzer and his immediate following, and
> throw yourselves completely onto our mercy, our
> treatment of you . . . will be such that you may yet,
> if circumstances permit, find favour in our eyes.[86]

With fear sapping their resolve the peasants did not
waver. Müntzer preached apocalypse and prophesied
victory unscathed for God's elect. As the morning wore
on an atmospheric halo formed a ring around the sun.
That was taken by the rebels as an infallible portent of
God's blessing since they saw it as a rainbow, the emblem
blazoned on the flag of Müntzer's Eternal League of God.
But as the sun reached its zenith, the princes fired their
opening salvoes into the peasants' ranks. The first men
fell; panic seized the rest; a wild stampede down the
hillside followed. Those rebels who were not crushed to
death were mown down like poppies by the knights on
horseback. Six thousand perished; six hundred were
taken prisoner; a handful managed to escape, amongst
them Müntzer. The Peasants' War in central Germany
had foundered in a bloody rout.

Müntzer took refuge in a house in Frankenhausen,

where he hid beneath the bedclothes and feigned infirmity. History has mocked this apparent cowardice; in truth, he was bewildered and in shock, for he clung to a precious but incriminating sack of letters and papers which at once revealed his identity to soldiers searching the house. Müntzer was dragged off to Ernst von Mansfeld's fortress at Heldrungen for interrogation. What he confessed, at first voluntarily and then on the rack, tells as much about his inquisitors as about the prisoner himself.

The Catholic officials were clearly concerned to have him repent his false religious doctrines before giving details of the rebels' organisation and aims, for the first two articles treated his understanding of the Roman Mass. His confession, including those passages uttered under torture, was rapidly disseminated in handwritten copies and then in print – as far afield as the Swabian League and Nuremberg[87] – in a deliberate attempt to discredit and defame him. Yet the confession veers so wildly between statements of principle and trivial details unintelligible to outsiders that it is hard to know what impact it can have made. Much of the questioning was addressed to issues of immediate concern to Ernst von Mansfeld, and several of Müntzer's replies were scarcely calculated to place Luther or the Protestant cause in a favourable light. The jumbled artlessness of the confession may well betoken its general trustworthiness, though one crucial statement – 'that the castles are grievously oppressive and bristling with compulsory dues and other forms of exploitation of their subjects' – is only contained in the edition printed at Leipzig, not the manuscript. Apart from his initial testimony on the Mass Müntzer's distinctive theological voice rarely breaks through: the confession in the main deals with the planning of secular rebellion. Only in the so-called 'Recantation' of 17 May is he compelled to forswear his doctrines, but the authenticity of that document is rendered even more suspect by his farewell letter the same day to the people of Mühlhausen. In it Müntzer points unerringly to the cause of the debâcle:

> Dear brothers, it is quite crucial that the sort of disaster which befell the men at Frankenhausen should not be your lot, too; there is no doubt of its root cause: that everyone was more concerned with his own self-interest than in bringing justice to the Christian people. Therefore make a clear distinction between these; see to it that you bring no further harm on yourselves. . . . I have often warned you that the only way to escape the punishment of God . . . is to recognise what harm will ensue, and it always can be recognised.[88]

But whilst he adjures them to 'shun all gatherings and disturbances and seek the mercy of the princes', Müntzer nowhere abjures his own beliefs. If the people 'step forward with the clear, unwavering righteousness of God', they cannot come to harm. Meanwhile the tyrants will persist as God's instruments of mortification to the faithful until the world is properly enlightened and the time of the harvest is finally at hand. His mistake was to associate the elect with the common folk, the poor, the materially oppressed.

The 'Recantation', by contrast, testifies to fundamental error; Müntzer admitted to the wantonness of his rebellion and to a false understanding of the Mass, and allowed himself to be reconciled to the Catholic faith. If Müntzer capitulated so abjectly, it can only have been when broken by torture. To one for whom the true knowledge of faith lay in the abyss of the soul the outward form of the Mass may no longer have meant much,[89] if indeed it ever had.

Müntzer was kept at Heldrungen for a week whilst the princes, blithely disregarding the niceties of the imperial constitution, invoked their right of protection to subjugate Mühlhausen. On 22 May Pfeiffer and his followers, three hundred strong, fled from the city, hoping to find cover amongst the Franconian peasants as they headed southwards towards Basel. Near Eisenach Pfeiffer was captured and led back to Mühlhausen. On 25 May the city opened its gates to admit the victorious princely troops. Müntzer was then brought to their headquarters at duke George of Saxony's camp at Görmar. On 27 May the two preachers were taken out into the field for execution. Müntzer's last hours belong to legend, but there is no reason to doubt the report that he warned the princes to deal gently with their subjects and to study diligently the first and second books of Kings. Broken in mind and body he could barely stammer the creed. Then the sword fell. The head and body of both preachers were stuck on pikestaffs for display. Despite his last entreaties, Müntzer's wife Ottilie von Gersen was not given custody of his property, and her own requests to the council of Mühlhausen were not honoured. In mid-August she petitioned duke George for help, seemingly to no avail.[90] After September 1525 no further trace of her or her offspring survives.

Without Müntzer a popular uprising would still have engulfed Thuringia, but his creation of the Eternal League of God in Mühlhausen and his leadership of the rebel army at Frankenhausen lent a unique dimension to the Peasants' War in central Germany, as he strove to harness secular rebellion to a theological revolution. Yet at the moment of truth his support faltered and evaporated. That Müntzer was obliged to issue desperate appeals to a variety of communities throughout Thuringia is in itself testimony that his attempt to launch a mass revolutionary movement had failed. The blame for this fiasco has

usually been laid at the door of the rebel troops themselves who were allegedly too hidebound by local interests to share Müntzer's overarching vision of a purified
and perfect Christian commonwealth of the elect. This
view seems to be confirmed by the fact that Müntzer's
following remained securely loyal where his influence had
been most protracted and intense. In Allstedt and
environs, where according to Zeiß half the inhabitants at
the end of April had already flocked to Frankenhausen,
the Saxon official reported a mere three days later that
the entire populace, barring a dozen or so, had by then
rallied to the rebels' cause.[91] In neighbouring Sangerhausen, whose population had fled in droves to Allstedt
for protection the previous summer, the godly league of
6 May spanning town and country sent fifteen hundred
men to the Frankenhausen army.

In the Mansfeld lands, by contrast, whose miners
formed the backbone of Müntzer's Christian league in
July 1524, only a trickle of support found its way to Frankenhausen, despite the active campaign against secular
and ecclesiastical lordships in northern Thuringia which
they waged at the beginning of May in defiance of assurances given to count Albrecht. But the traditional Marxist
view of the miners as the spearhead of Müntzer's 'party'
vastly overestimates their potential as a early proletarian
class: their objective situation created barriers to an active
alliance with the peasantry which Müntzer's impassioned
rhetoric could not overcome.[92]

What vision of a new society was Müntzer in fact
prepared to offer the Thuringian rebels? Under torture he
confessed that 'he had launched the rising with the aim
of making all Christians equal and of expelling and doing
to death the princes and gentry who refused to support
the Gospel', according to which 'all things are to be held
in common and distribution should be to each according
to his need, as occasion arises'.[93] But this primitive distrib-

utivism fell well short of radical socialist egalitarianism, as his statements on secular authority make plain. In the *Constitutional Draft* he had envisaged a Christian brother-hood, in which lordship (a hierarchy of government) would be retained – as the provisions for the election of kings, princes and territorial lords demonstrate; in that brotherhood, according to the fourth Frankenhausen article, all noble titles were to be abolished, though the lord's property was to be restituted if they upheld the Gospel, whereupon they should also receive expropriated monastic lands. In his voluntary confession, moreover, he even acknowledged a differentiation of noble privileges according to rank: on public occasions a prince was to be permitted an escort of eight horses, a count four, and a knight or gentleman merely two.[94] Müntzer admittedly advocated the destruction of the lords' castles (and acted thereupon in the Eichsfeld campaign), from which the material oppression of the common folk derived, but he was willing, it appears, to follow Pfeiffer in retaining one castle as the administrative seat of each district.[95] On that basis, Müntzer revealed, the rebel armies intended to capture all the territory within a radius of fifty miles of Mühlhausen, stretching well into the landgraviate of Hessen.[96] Whether this region was to be constituted as a Christian commonwealth independent of princely juris-diction under the protection of Mühlhausen as an imperial free city is uncertain, but by no means improbable.

Although Müntzer ultimately fleshed out his skeletal *Constitutional Draft* with ideas which point towards a theo-cratic republic in which certain distinctions of rank (if not of title) and private property were to be preserved within a general framework of the commonweal and the normative authority of God's word, his blueprint was clearly intended as provisional. It covered the interim in which the kingdom of the Elect would reign supreme before the ultimate true kingdom of God. In that sense, therefore,

he had no real 'theory of society'.[97] That, in turn, accounts
for Müntzer's apparent vagueness towards secular rulers:
whether they should be killed as godless tyrants, expropriated and deposed, or reinstated as common brothers
depended less upon their outward exercise of power and
authority than upon their inward responsiveness to the
message of true faith. That attitude above all determined
the princes' fate, as it did for all mankind: election or
damnation. To seek to categorise Müntzer's view of
secular authority as either 'revolutionary' or 'moderate'
becomes thus arbitrary and otiose, for lordship was no
longer property but responsibility.[98]

How far the common folk were capable of empathy
for Müntzer's vision remains a matter of dispute. In his
confession the precept of Christian equality (in the Latin
tag *'omnia sunt communia'*) was attached specifically to the
aims of his Allstedt league, yet one of its members, Claus
Rautenzweig could only mutter under interrogation that
'they should love each other as brothers',[99] a pretty
shallow rendering of Müntzer's intentions. The only echo
amongst the peasantry of the slogan *'omnia sunt communia'*
crops up in a complaint by Hans and Hartmann von
Goldacker, lords of Ufhoven by Langensalza, at the end
of April that their subjects had returned drunken and
incoherent from the peasant army, 'demanding variously
to have this or that, since everything is in common,
although they have not brought the articles with them'.
In fact, the articles transpired to be the 'Twelve Articles
which the Black Forest peasants have printed', that is to
say those of Upper Swabia, which called for the
communal ownership and usufruct of land, rather than
the out-of-hand abolition of seigneurial authority *tout
court*.[100] Against that must be set the action of the Sangerhausen peasants in forming a godly league with the
townsfolk on Müntzerite principles and their subsequent
contribution to the ranks of the Frankenhausen rebels.

However, the purpose of their league was not quite what it appeared. When the two thousand countryfolk assembled in the town on 3 May they compelled the council and the albertine official, Melchior von Kutzleben, to accede to demands which turned out once again to be the Twelve Articles of Upper Swabia. The Sangerhausen peasants, in other words, had adopted the *form* of Müntzer's leagues in order to cloak 'creaturely' demands whose *content* was predicated upon their specific agrarian grievances and which had nothing to do with Müntzer's concept of the league's function.[101] Nor is that the only instance. In the last week of April 1525 the 'Evangelic Brotherly League' in the territory of the counts of Schwarzburg urged the town of Blankenburg to adopt the Twelve Articles.[102]

The prevalence of the Upper Swabian articles throughout Thuringia is all the more striking given that certain demands, notably for the abolition of serfdom, had little bearing on local conditions, as the ducal Saxon councillor, Dr Otto von Pack, shrewdly noted.[103] At least part of the attraction which the Twelve Articles with their religious preamble and scriptural glosses exerted must, therefore, have been ideological: in that case they could provide an alternative focus of inspiration to Müntzer's own theological vision. Müntzer seems to have acknowledged as much in his confession for when his own followers in the Mühlhausen-Thuringian army were encamped at Ebeleben before the start of the Eichsfeld campaign they vented their grievances against a local lord, Apel von Ebeleben, which were 'set out in various articles not known to him. They were partly the Twelve Articles of the Black Forest peasants and partly others'.[104]

The same is true, of course, of the Frankenhausen Articles, which conflated elements of the Twelve Articles and demands embraced by Müntzer and Pfeiffer. Beyond their rather sketchy paraphrase, however, it is evident from the account of events which Hans Zeiß sent to his cousin, Christoph Meinhard, in Eisleben on 5 May that certain of Müntzer's ideas had taken root amongst the rebels well before he reached the camp at Frankenhausen. The secular lords, Zeiß reported, should be stripped of their authority and obliged to stand before the rebels as equals (only the Saxon elector was to be allowed to retain his dignity and office); the nobles should be granted a mounted escort commensurate with their rank; they should only be reinstated on condition that they uphold the Gospel; their castles should be razed to the ground; they might be admitted to the rebel host as common brothers.[105] Zeiß's letter to Meinhard, which betrays a much warmer sympathy for Müntzer's cause than the run of official reports to his Saxon overlords,[106] nevertheless makes plain that Müntzer's was not the only voice to be raised as the rebellion gathered pace:

> It is not the case that Müntzer is a captain or the leader of the troop, as people say. He is nothing other than the Mühlhauseners' preacher. In the troop there are also many other preachers, who preach the Gospel according to Luther's interpretation. They pay no particular heed to Müntzer, even though he has committed himself to the game afoot in his letter [to Allstedt].[107]

These remarks should not be construed to imply that Müntzer faced concerted opposition from a wing of the Frankenhausen troop less radical than himself;[108] rather, they may reflect a deliberate emphasis on Müntzer's theological and pastoral function by Zeiß, eager to shield him from accusations of wilful insurrection. Yet they confirm the overwhelming impression which the evidence of the rebels' actions, organisation and aims at every turn conveys – that the links between Müntzer's theological revolution and the mass of the peasants' aspirations and demands were fitful, fragile and fortuitous. In the end the rebels saw well enough that Müntzer's religious ideology was inadequate to their cause: it supplied the framework for organised rebellion through the Christian leagues, but it could not offer any detailed programme for those leagues to adopt. Only the lesser townsfolk, those whose grievances least reflected entrenched social and economic relations of production, can be said to have embraced Müntzer's essentially amorphous vision in full measure. The peasantry, by contrast, remained an uneasy ally in both its mentality and aspirations. The mass support with which Müntzer reckoned never materialised.

Yet the 'legend' of Thomas Müntzer, which was intended to defame him, continued to exercise a powerful fascination not only upon his contemporaries but also in the generations to come. His name became the totem of struggles for emancipation from the age of the Enlightenment onwards. Yet the further removed those who invoked his name were from the religious turmoil of the sixteenth century, the more Müntzer's transcendent theological vision was pushed into the background. At first he was portrayed as the champion of personal freedom and dignity, then as the hero of the common people, and latterly as the pioneer of a communist society. In all these cases those who used his name could do so with impunity, secure in the knowledge that their mentor could not gainsay them from the grave.

Notes

1. The evidence is critically reviewed in Günter Vogler, *Nürnberg 1524/25. Studien zur Geschichte der reformatorischen und sozialen Bewegung in der Reichsstadt* (Berlin, 1982), 213–32.

2. Bubenheimer, 'Luther – Karlstadt – Müntzer', 62.
3. E 631 ff.
4. CW 433 f.
5. James M. Stayer, 'Radikaler Frühzwinglianismus. Balthasar Hubmaier, Fabers "Ursach" und die Programme der Bauern', *Mennonitische Geschichtsblätter*, XLII (1985), 45.
6. QBK 235–6.
7. Ibid. 232 (my translation).
8. Cf. CW 280 ff.
9. Cf. Torsten Bergsten, *Balthasar Hubmaier. Anabaptist theologian and martyr*, ed. W. R. Estep, Jr (Valley Forge, Pa., 1978), 218 ff.
10. Cf. Tom Scott, 'Reformation and Peasants' War in Waldshut and environs: a structural analysis', part II, *Archiv für Reformationsgeschichte*, LXX (1979), 147.
11. Cf. Peter Blickle, *Die Revolution von 1525*, 2nd edn (Munich/Vienna, 1981), 227, n. 7.
12. E 659; Gottfried Seebaß, *Artikelbrief, Bundesordnung und Verfassungsentwurf. Studien zu drei zentralen Dokumenten des südwestdeutschen Bauernkrieges* (Abhandlungen der Heidelberger Akademie der Wissenschaften, phil.-hist. Klasse, LXXXVIII, 1) (Heidelberg, 1988), 167–8.
13. Cf. Stayer, 'Radikaler Frühzwinglianismus', 45.
14. E 661.
15. S II 132.
16. W 92.
17. James M. Stayer, *Anabaptists and the Sword*, new edn (Lawrence, Kan., 1976), 76; cf. idem, 'Radikaler Frühzwinglianismus', 55.
18. Cf. Seebaß, *Artikelbrief, Bundesordnung und Verfassungsentwurf*, 165 ff., n. 77 f.
19. S II 89; QBK 236.
20. Cf. Günter Vogler, 'Tendenzen der sozialen und politischen Programmatik im deutschen Bauernkrieg. Ein Vergleich mit Gaismairs Tiroler Landesordnung' in Fridolin Dörrer (ed.), *Die Bauernkriege und Michael Gaismair* (Veröffentlichungen des Tiroler Landesarchivs, II) Innsbruck, 1982), 108. This modifies his earlier view that

the 'castle article' demonstrates the application of revolutionary violence. Günter Vogler, 'Schlösserartikel und weltlicher Bann im deutschen Bauernkrieg' in Gerhard Brendler and Adolf Laube (eds), *Der Deutsche Bauernkrieg 1524/25. Geschichte – Tradition – Lehren* (Akademie der Wissenschaften der DDR: Schriften des Zentralinstituts für Geschichte, LVII) (Berlin, 1977), 120.

21. Seebaß, *Artikelbrief, Bundesordnung und Verfassungsentwurf*, 150 ff.
22. Ibid. 50 ff.
23. In his letter to the Church of Mühlhausen, for example. CW 133. E 669 believes that it is a concept not found at all in Müntzer!
24. Cf. Winfried Eberhard, ' "Gemeiner Nutzen" als oppositionelle Leitvorstellung im Spätmittelalter' in Manfred Gerwing and Godehard Ruppert (eds), *Renovatio et Reformatio. Wider das Bild vom 'finsteren' Mittelalter. Festschrift für Ludwig Hödl zum 60. Geburtstag* (Münster, 1985), 195–214, esp. 202 ff.
25. CW 457.
26. See above 76.
27. Scott, 'Reformation and Peasants' War', part II, 148 ff.
28. S I 140. Cf. Peter Blickle *et al.*, 'Zürichs Anteil am deutschen Bauernkrieg. Die Vorstellung des göttlichen Rechts im Klettgau', *Zeitschrift für die Geschichte des Oberrheins*, cxxxiii (1985), 93.
29. QBK 96–7; E 642.
30. Peter Blickle, 'Das göttliche Recht der Bauern und die göttliche Gerechtigkeit der Reformatoren', *Archiv für Kulturgeschichte*, lxviii (1986), 351–69.
31. Blickle *et al.*, 'Zürichs Anteil', 91 ff.
32. Blickle, 'Das göttlich Recht', 363 and n. 51.
33. CW 438.
34. AGBM II 66.
35. See the instructive essay by Heinz Schilling, 'Aufstandsbewegungen in der Stadtbürgerlichen Gesellschaft des Alten Reiches. Die Vorgeschichte des Münsteraner Täuferreichs, 1525 bis 1534' in Hans-Ulrich Wehler (ed.), *Der Deutsche Bauernkrieg 1524–1526 (Gesch-*

ichte und Gesellschaft. Zeitschrift für historische Sozialwissenschaft, Sonderheft I) (Göttingen, 1975), 193–238.

36. G II 79–80.
37. Ibid. 80–1; QBK 497.
38. Müntzer's harangue is further indication that a league had not been formed the previous September. Scott, ' "Volksreformation" ', 206.
39. AGBM II 67; G II 82. The dating is most uncertain. There was also wild talk that the Franconian and Black Forest peasants were poised to intervene!
40. According to the Mühlhausen chronicle, QBK 497. The surviving list of names numbers only 820, with numerous repetitions! Cf. Leisering, 'Anhänger Thomas Müntzers', 35.
41. Cf. Scott, ' "Volksreformation" ', 208, n. 79.
42. Ibid. 206–7.
43. Staatsarchiv Dresden, Loc. 9135, Acta den Aufruhr zu Mühlhausen betreffend, I, fo. 44 r.
44. Leisering, 'Anhänger Thomas Müntzers', 16–17.
45. In the surviving register the plebeians and peasant burghers are clearly underrepresented. Ibid. 20ff.
46. B 83–4 and n. 96.
47. CW 137.
48. Cf. ibid. 140.
49. LW, vol. XLVI, 19–20.
50. QBK 498.
51. B 195 ff. Cf. most recently Tom Scott, 'Martin Luther und der Bauernkrieg in Mitteldeutschland' in Horst Bartel, Gerhard Brendler *et al.* (eds), *Martin Luther. Leistung und Erbe* (Berlin, 1986), 152–7.
52. LW, vol. XLVI, 49.
53. Cf. Mark U. Edwards, Jr, *Luther and the false brethren* (Stanford, Cal., 1975), 67–8.
54. CW 140f.
55. Ibid. 141.
56. Ibid. 142.
57. Ibid. 142.
58. Ibid. 143.
59. Ibid. 144.

60. B 114 ff.
61. Cf. Reinhard Jordan, 'Pfeifers und Münzers Zug in das Eichsfeld und die Verwüstung der Klöster und Schlösser', *Zeitschrift des Vereins für thüringische Geschichte und Altertumskunde*, new series XIV (1904), 46 ff.
62. AGBM II 230.
63. Ibid. 453.
64. Ibid. 383. Cf. the detailed investigation of the relations between the two preachers in Ludwig Rommel, 'Heinrich Pfeiffer und Thomas Müntzer oder die Geschichte einer Legende', *Jahrbuch für Geschichte des Feudalismus*, XI (1987), 203–21, esp, 210 ff., 214.
65. See above 138.
66. CW 145.
67. Ibid. 146.
68. Ibid. 148.
69. Ibid. 148.
70. Ibid. 149.
71. B 184 ff.; E 722 ff.
72. G II 298–9.
73. QBK 536; AGBM II 383.
74. Ibid. 753.
75. Cf. Gerhard Günther, 'Bemerkungen zum Thema "Thomas Müntzer und Heinrich Pfeiffer in Mühlhausen" ', in Gerhard Heitz *et al.* (eds), *Der Bauer im Klassenkampf. Studien zur Geschichte des deutschen Bauernkrieges und der bäuerlichen Klassenkämpfe im Spätfeudalismus* (Berlin, 1975), 180.
76. G II 336, n. 1.
77. CW 436.
78. B 179.
79. Siegfried Hoyer, *Das Militärwesen im deutschen Bauernkrieg 1524–1526* (Militärhistorische Studien, new series XVI) (Berlin, 1975), 158.
80. CW 157.
81. Ibid. 156.
82. Cf. Scribner, 'Civic unity in Erfurt', 45 f.
83. Cf. the interpretation in E 764–5.
84. R 244. Philip of Hessen brought troops up at the rear to

cut off any escape through the woods of the Kyffhäuser mountain range. Hoyer, *Militärwesen*, 160.

85.   CW 159. To construe this appeal, as does Maron, as a rejection of Müntzer's apocalyptic vision ignores the context in which it was written. Cf. Gottfried Maron, 'Thomas Müntzer als Theologe des Gerichts. Das "Urteil" – ein Schlüsselbegriff seines Denkens' in Abraham Friesen and Hans-Jürgen Goertz (eds), *Thomas Müntzer* (*Wege der Forschung*, vol. CDXCI) (Darmstadt, 1978), 380, n. 229a.

86.   CW 160.

87.   Information kindly supplied by Prof. Ulrich Bubenheimer.

88.   CW 160 f.

89.   W 110–11.

90.   CW 459 f.

91.   AGBM II 162, 181.

92.   Scott, ' "Volksreformation" ', 212–13; Adolf Laube, 'Zum Problem des Bündnisses von Bergarbeitern und Bauern im deutschen Bauernkrieg' in Heitz *et al.*, *Bauer im Klassenkampf*, 105 ff.

93.   CW 436 f.

94.   Ibid. 434.

95.   Compare ibid. 434 and 436.

96.   Ibid. 437. The ten miles mentioned in the German text approximate to the fifty English statute miles I have cited.

97.   R 302.

98.   W 103.

99.   AGBM II 453.

100.   G II 198–200; Scott, ' "Volksreformation" ', 211.

101.   G II 164 f., 167 ff.; Scott, ' "Volksreformation" ', 212.

102.   QBK 504.

103.   G II 171 ff.

104.   CW 435.

105.   QBK 512.

106.   Cf. Held, 'Zeiß und Müntzer', 1074, 1089.

107.   QBK 513.

108.   Cf. E 737 against B 165.

Conclusion

History has remembered only the violent Müntzer, wielding the sword and heaping salvoes of abuse upon his enemies. It has forgotten the more gentle Müntzer, the theologian steeped in mystical resignation, the pastor ministering to his flock, the first liturgist of Protestantism. The 'legend' of Müntzer constructed by the Wittenberg orthodoxy of Luther, Melanchthon and Johann Agricola seized deliberately upon the image of the fanatical insurrectionary in the Peasants' War, and belittled or ignored his theological erudition, his intellectual creativity, and, above all, his earnest and engaged humanity. Yet Müntzer grew from the same soil as did the Evangelical reformers: he absorbed many of the same theological influences and shared Luther's eschatological conviction that the Last Days had dawned. His mysticism was not so far removed from Karlstadt's; his attack on the burdens borne by the common people echoed that of Jakob Strauß. Even where he parted company from Wittenberg Müntzer did not become isolated in a theological wilderness, but remained a pilgrim whose intellectual journey brought him close to the shores of Reformed Protestantism in South-West Germany and Switzerland. His attitude towards worldly authority, for instance, finds parallels in Huldrych Zwingli; his spiritualism was not entirely dissimilar to Martin Bucer's.

Despite the caricature of his opponents, Müntzer's immediate legacy did not, in any case, altogether neglect his reforming achievement. His liturgies were adopted by the congregations of Erfurt and Wolfenbüttel in 1525, despite Luther's attempts to halt their printing. In Allstedt itself, the Saxon ecclesiastical visitors found to their vexation much of Müntzer's order of service still in use in 1533.[1] Several of his hymns continued to be sung, albeit put down to an 'anonymous' composer. The most striking fact about Müntzer's revolutionary theology, however, was that it did not die with him, despite the debâcle at Frankenhausen. On the contrary, it had a profound influence upon two Anabaptist leaders who had fought there by his side. One was Hans Römer from Eisenach, who defended Müntzer after his execution and, fired by an undimmed eschatological fervour, planned to launch a fresh rebellion in 1527 which would herald the imminent end of the world. The other was Hans Hut, who played a leading role in the spread of spiritualist Anabaptism in southern Germany. In contrast to Römer, Hut eventually abjured his commitment to violence but retained an apocalyptic scheme which was heavily indebted to Müntzer. How far they or later Anabaptists fully comprehended the profundity and complexity of Müntzer's thought remains a matter of debate.[2]

Undoubtedly the stumbling-block to a proper understanding of Müntzer, then as now, lies in his commitment to violent rebellion. How could a man so imbued with the spirit of mystical resignation come to take up the sword against the godless? Yet revolution is immanent in his theology from its first maturing around 1520. The re-establishment of the order of creation, as conceived in the *German Theology*, the mystical treatise which Müntzer had read in Luther's edition of 1518, that is to say, both as an order embracing God *and* creation as well as an order implanted by God *in* creation itself,[3] required and implied

not only the restoration of the 'inner order', the unity of
God and man, but equally the transformation of the 'outer
order', the structure of worldly society – indeed, of all
human existence – so that it likewise became conformed
to God's will.[4] When Müntzer linked that mystical conviction to an apocalyptic reading of history, it catalysed into
a theology of revolution. The clasp which united the
mystical, apocalyptic and biblical strands of his theology
was the doctrine of predestination, the view of the world
as cloven between godly and godless, elect and damned.[5]
The instrument by which Müntzer then sought to convert
his religious theory into revolutionary practice was the
Christian league, conceived as a new covenant between
God and man. With that sense of mission Müntzer strode
into battle at the head of the Eternal League of God, as
'God's servant against the godless'.

In the face of adversity and persecution Müntzer saw
the ranks of the godless swell as the members of the true
elect diminished. Gradually he came to associate only
the materially oppressed with the poor in spirit, those
uniquely capable of achieving true faith, just as he began
to equate all government as such with the ungodly and
sinful world. 'Faith' and 'world' became mutually contradictory and exclusive.[6] Müntzer's apocalyptic gave him
assurance, however, that the handful of the elect would
vanquish the legions of the damned. At that point
Müntzer's grip on reality faltered. So obsessed had he
become by his vision of the world, almost Manichaean in
its dualism, that he could no longer conceive of the world
as anything but evil and worthy of destruction.[7] His
doctrine of necessary suffering and abnegation came, in
the end, perilously close to abjuring God's creation.

Against that background it is not hard to see why
Müntzer was so reluctant to offer a blueprint for a new
and purified Christian society. The most that he was
willing to propose was guidelines for the temporary sover-

eignty of the elect. As a consequence, certain fundamental themes which shaped and stiffened his commitment to rebellion remained rudimentary and unresolved. It was left to other manifestos of the Peasants' War to give them sharper contours: the stark opposition of selfishness and the common good is the leitmotiv of Hans Hergot's *On the New Transformation of a Christian Life*;[8] the vision of a theocratic commonwealth is set forth in Michael Gaismair's *Tirolean Constitution* of 1526.[9] The *Constitutional Draft*, with its 'certain articles on how one should govern', appears, by contrast, shadowy and embryonic. During the Last Days of the world the Bible, for Müntzer always a book of laws, was to be the arbiter of human affairs, but how it was to be applied he did not answer. What mattered to him was who used the Bible: for to the elect true illumination would be given.[10] What Müntzer promised his followers, to adapt the words of another revolutionary in a very different age, was 'freedom, not the ultimate freedom that all Christians desire, but the freedom to achieve it'.[11] For Müntzer, ultimate freedom was not his, but God's, to bestow.

Notes

1. R 322.
2. Friesen, 'Müntzer and the Anabaptists', 151 ff., 158 f.
3. Hans-Jürgen Goertz, 'The mystic with the hammer: Thomas Müntzer's theological basis for revolution', *Mennonite Quarterly Review*, L (1976), 96–7.
4. Idem, *Innere und Äußere Ordnung*, 133.
5. Gordon Rupp, ' "True History": Martin Luther and Thomas Müntzer' in Derek Beales and Geoffrey Best (eds), *History, society and the Churches: Essays in honour of Owen Chadwick* (Cambridge, 1985), 84.
6. Goertz, 'Mystic with the hammer', 101.
7. Ibid. 108.

8. Cf. Blickle, *Revolution of 1525*, 150–4.

9. Cf. most recently Giorgio Politi, 'I sette sigilli della "Landes-ordnung". Un programma rivoluzionario del primo Cinquecento fra equivoci e mito', *Annali dell' Istituto storico italo-germanico in Trento*, XII (1986), 9–86.

10. Rudolf Mau, 'Müntzers Verständnis von der Bibel' in Christoph Demke (ed.), *Thomas Müntzer. Anfragen an Theologie und Kirche* (Berlin, 1977), 34–5.

11. Michael Collins in the Treaty Debate in Dáil Eireann on 19 December 1921: 'It gives us freedom, not the ultimate freedom that all nations desire and develop to, but the freedom to achieve it.' *Official Report* of the *Debate on the Treaty between Great Britain and Ireland signed on the 6th December 1921* (Dublin, n.d. [1922]), 32.

Chronology

1489 (?)	Müntzer born at Stolberg (Harz)
1506	Study at Leipzig (?)
1512	Study at Frankfurt an der Oder
1512/13 (?)	Assistant teacher in Aschersleben and Halle. Forms 'league' against archbishop Ernest of Magdeburg
1514, 6 May	Chantry priest at St Michael's, Brunswick
1515/16	Provost and schoolmaster at canonesses' house at Frose
1517, Winter	Attends lectures at Wittenberg
1518/19 (?)	Visits Rothenburg ob der Tauber

1519

January	In Leipzig
Easter	Deputy preacher at Jüterbog
June	Attends Leipzig disputation
December–April 1520	Confessor to Cistercian nunnery at Beuditz
circa 1520	Death of Müntzer's mother

1520

May	Preacher at St Mary's, Zwickau
1 October	Preacher at St Catherine's, Zwickau

1521

16 April	Flight from Zwickau
Spring	Visits Žatec (Saaz)
June	Journey to Prague
1 November	*Prague Manifesto* (shorter German version)
(November)	Latin version
25 November	Longer German version
December	Flight from Prague

1522

New Year	In Erfurt
Easter	Visits Stolberg
July (?)	In Nordhausen
November	Attends disputation in Weimar
Christmas	Chaplaincy at St George's nunnery, Glaucha near Halle

1523

March	Pastor of St John's, Allstedt
June (?)	Marriage to former nun, Ottilie von Gersen
Summer (?)	First Allstedt league of 30 members
Summer	*German Church Service; German Evangelical Mass*
18 July	*An Open Letter to his Dear Brothers in Stolberg*
September	First conflict with count Ernst von Mansfeld
November	Disputation in Allstedt castle
Winter	*Order and Explanation of the German Church Service at Allstedt*
Winter–New Year 1524	*Protestation or Proposition; On Counterfeit Faith*

1524

24 March	Destruction of Chapel at Mallerbach
Easter	Birth of Müntzer's son
11 June	Arrest of councillor, Ziliax Knaut
13 June	Emergency defence ordinance in Allstedt
14 June	Allstedt on the alert; Müntzer calls for league to defend the Gospel
13 July	*Sermon to the Princes (Interpretation of the Second Chapter of Daniel)*
24 July	Formation of Christian League or Covenant
31 July–1 August	Interrogation of Müntzer and Allstedt councillors in Weimar
July–August	*A Manifest Exposé of False Faith* (abbreviated version as *The Testimony of the First Chapter of the Gospel of Luke*); *A Highly Provoked Vindication and a Refutation of the Unspiritual Soft-Living Flesh in Wittenberg*
3 August (?)	Enforced closure of printing-works in Allstedt and dissolution of Christian League
7 August	Flight from Allstedt
mid-August	Arrival in Mühlhausen
early September (?)	Müntzer's wife, son and clerk follow him to Mühlhausen
19–26 September	Week-long crisis in Mühlhausen
22/23 September (?)	Eleven Mühlhausen Articles
27 September	Expulsion of Müntzer and Heinrich Pfeiffer from Mühlhausen
early October (?)	Visits Hans Hut in Bibra (?)
October–November (?)	In Nuremberg; printing of *A Manifest Exposé of False Faith*; confiscation

late November–early December (?)	Printing in Nuremberg of *A Highly Provoked Vindication*; confiscation
December	Return of Pfeiffer to Mühlhausen
early December (?)	In Basel; meeting with Oecolampadius and Hugwald
December–New Year 1525 (?)	In Klettgau and Hegau; composition of 'some articles, drawn from the Gospel, on how one should govern'

1525

February (?)	Temporary arrest in Fulda
late February	Return to Mühlhausen
28 February	Rector of St Mary's, Mühlhausen
9 March	Muster of Mühlhausen's militia
16 March	Citizenry summoned to St Mary's; election of Eternal Council
17 March	Installation of Eternal Council
late March–early April (?)	Formation of Eternal League of God
9–15 April	Introduction of the Reformation in Mühlhausen
mid-April	Peasant rebellion in western Thuringia (Werra valley troop)
11–12 April	Joint strategy of suppression agreed by princes at Naumburg
26 April	Müntzer's and Pfeiffer's march to Langensalza
26/27 April	Müntzer's open letter to his followers in Allstedt ('Manifesto to the Miners')
27 April	Sack of abbey of Volkenroda
27–29 April	Formation of Mühlhausen-Thuringian troop
late April	Luther's *Admonition to Peace: A*

	Reply to the Twelve Articles of the Peasants in Swabia
late April–early May	Luther's preaching tour of western Saxony and Thuringia; formation of Frankenhausen (North Thuringian) troop
30 April–6 May	Campaign of Mühlhausen-Thuringian troop in the Eichsfeld
mid-May	Luther's *Against the Robbing and Murdering Hordes of Peasants*
11 May	March of Mühlhausen contingent under Müntzer to Frankenhausen
14 May	Attack by Brunswick-Hessian army on Frankenhausen rebels' camp repelled
15 May	Battle of Frankenhausen; 6000 rebels killed; Müntzer captured
16 May	Interrogation and torture in Heldrungen castle
17 May	'Recantation'
22 May	Flight of 300 rebels from Mühlhausen; Pfeiffer captured
25 May	Capitulation of Mühlhausen
27 May	Execution of Müntzer and Pfeiffer outside Mühlhausen's walls
late May	Luther's *A Shocking History and God's Judgement on Thomas Müntzer*
19 August	Supplication by Ottilie von Gersen to duke George of Saxony

Suggestions for Further Reading

A comprehensive survey of recent literature on Müntzer is contained in Tom Scott, 'From Polemic to Sobriety: Thomas Müntzer in Recent Research', *Journal of Ecclesiastical History*, xxxix (1988). In place of the many miscellaneous translations of Müntzer's tracts and letters see the fine critical edition in English: *The Collected Works of Thomas Müntzer*, ed. Peter Matheson (Edinburgh, 1988). The only full-length biography in English remains that of Eric W. Gritsch, *Reformer without a Church. The Life and Thought of Thomas Muentzer, 1488(?)–1525* (Philadelphia, 1967). Still stimulating is Gordon Rupp, 'Thomas Müntzer. The Reformer as Rebel' in idem, *Patterns of Reformation* (London, 1969), a masterpiece of sympathetic insight, now overtaken in several aspects of interpretation and detail.

The standard work in German is Walter Elliger, *Thomas Müntzer, Leben und Werk*, 2nd edn (Göttingen, 1975). A massive biography, offering many new insights, which remains wedded to a narrowly theological interpretation and a close dialectical relationship between Müntzer and Luther. In *Reformation als Revolution. Soziale Bewegung und religiöser Radikalismus in der deutschen Reformation* (Munich, 1977), part 2, Richard van Dülmen attempts a broad analytic setting in sociological terms, marred by excessive reliance upon Manfred Bensing (see below) and a careless reading of the sources. Hans-Jürgen Goertz, 'Thomas Müntzer. Revolutionary in a Mystical Spirit' in idem (ed.), *Profiles of Radical Reformers. Biographical Sketches from Thomas Müntzer to Paracelsus* (Kitchener, Ont./Scottdale, Pa., 1982) gives a useful introductory survey, enlightening on Müntzer's theological background.

Müntzer's theology

Apart from Goertz's survey (see above) see Steven E. Ozment, *Mysticism and Dissent. Religious Ideology and Social Protest in the Sixteenth Century* (New Haven/London, 1973), ch. 3, who concentrates on *A Manifest Exposé of False Faith*. Still the most penetrating analysis is Hans-Jürgen Goertz, *Innere und Äußere Ordnung in der Theologie Thomas Müntzers* (Studies in the History of Christian Thought, II) (Leiden, 1967), although the 'order of creation' is now known to have other roots than those suggested by him.

Luther and Müntzer

Gordon Rupp, ' "True History": Martin Luther and Thomas Müntzer' in Derek Beales and Geoffrey Best (eds), *History, Society and the Churches. Essays in Honour of Owen Chadwick* (Cambridge, 1985) is the envoi of a distinguished scholar, who places Müntzer in a wider intellectual context. Mark U. Edwards, Jr, *Luther and the False Brethren* (Stanford, Cal., 1975) gives a sane and balanced analysis which does not blindly accept the Lutheran position. The classic account, which stresses the differences rather than the similarities between the two reformers, is by Carl Hinrichs, *Luther und Müntzer. Ihre Auseinandersetzung über Obrigkeit und Widerstandsrecht* (Arbeiten zur Kirchengeschichte, XXIX), 2nd edn (Berlin, 1962). The most recent summary is by Eric W. Gritsch, 'Thomas Müntzer and Luther: A Tragedy of Errors', in Hans J. Hillerbrand (ed.), *Radical Tendencies in the Reformation: Divergent Perspectives* (Sixteenth Century Essays and Studies, IX) (Kirksville, Mo., 1988).

Müntzer and the Peasants' War

Hans-Jürgen Goertz, 'The Mystic with the Hammer. Thomas Müntzer's Theological Basis for Revolution', *Mennonite Quarterly Review*, L (1976) is a masterly essay which reconciles Müntzer's theology and revolutionary involvement. Manfred Bensing, *Thomas Müntzer und der Thüringer Aufstand 1525* (Leipziger Übersetzungen und Abhandlungen zum Mittelalter, series B III) (Berlin, 1966) provides an exhaustive East German account with a wealth of useful detail but often polemical and tendentious in interpretation. G. H. Williams, *The Radical Reformation* (Philadelphia, 1962), ch. 2 contains a summary based on the older literature. Tom Scott, 'The "Volksreformation" of Thomas Müntzer in Allstedt and Mühlhausen', *Journal of Ecclesiastical History*, XXXIV (1983) offers a reassessment of Müntzer's Christian leagues, the backbone of his active theological vision; certain details are now revised in the present work. Peter Blickle, *The Revolution of 1525. The German Peasants' War from a New Perspective* (Baltimore, Md/London, 1981), ch. 8 gives a thumbnail sketch of Müntzer's revolutionary theology. Idem, 'Gab es eine Volksreformation? Überlegungen zur begrifflichen Präzisierung der reformatorischen Bewegung' in Horst Bartel, Gerhard Brendler *et al.* (eds), *Martin Luther. Leistung und Erbe* (Berlin, 1986) advances an important critique of the Marxist concept of the 'people's Reformation', which argues that, in these terms, Müntzer's programme was unique neither to him nor to central Germany.

Müntzer and Anabaptism

Werner O. Packull, *Mysticism and the Early South-German-Austrian Anabaptist Movement* (Studies in Anabaptist and Mennonite History, XIX) (Scottdale, Pa./Kitchener, Ont., 1977) is a pioneering study which assigns Müntzer a relatively modest role. By contrast he is seen as crucial to Hans Hut, in particular, by Abraham Friesen, 'Thomas Müntzer and the Anabaptists', *Journal of Mennonite Studies*, IV (1986). James M. Stayer, *Anabaptists and the Sword*, new edn (Lawrence, Kan., 1976) offers useful comments on Müntzer's view of worldly authority. Wide-ranging extracts of important articles in abbreviated translation are contained in idem and Werner O. Packull (eds), *The Anabaptists and Thomas Müntzer* (Dubuque, Iowa, 1980).

The Historiography of Müntzer

Abraham Friesen, *Reformation and Utopia. The Marxist Interpretation of the Reformation and its Antecedents* (Veröffentlichungen des Instituts für europäische Geschichte, Mainz, LXXI) (Wiesbaden, 1974) is a problematic account of the Marxist approach to the Reformation, especially to the concept of an 'early bourgeois revolution', which presents an analysis of works no longer necessarily normative amongst East German scholars. Max Steinmetz, *Das Müntzerbild von Martin Luther bis Friedrich Engels* (Leipziger Übersetzungen und Abhandlungen zum Mittelalter, series B IV) (Berlin, 1971) remains the classic East German account.

Index